THE
BEAUX'
STRATAGEM
BY
GEORGE FARQUHAR

EDITED BY
VINCENT F. HOPPER
GERALD B. LAHEY
New York University

WITH A NOTE ON
THE STAGING BY
George L. Hersey
Yale University

ILLUSTRATED
BY
Keogh

BARRON'S EDUCATIONAL SERIES, INC.
GREAT NECK, NEW YORK

THEATRE CLASSICS FOR THE MODERN READER

To reproduce the values and effects of the theatre on the printed page is the ambitious aim of this series of the classics of the stage. Although good plays have always been read as well as acted, few playwrights before the era of Ibsen and Shaw have ever written with any public other than the theatre audience sharply in their minds. In consequence, the reader of older plays is usually required to supply his own visualizing of the staging and his own interpretation of stage action and even the manner of the delivery of the lines themselves. Frequently he is also required to put up with abbreviations and other space-saving printing devices.

This modern reader's edition of theatre classics vitalizes the outstanding plays of the past with the kind of eye-pleasing text and the kinds of reading and acting guides to which today's reader is accustomed in good published editions of twentieth century dramas. The text itself has not been altered except for occasional modernizations of spelling and punctuation (common to all modern editions of earlier works) and the rare use of italics for emphasis when the reading of a line is not immediately clear. Essentially, that is, the author's text is as he wrote it. Added to it are descriptions of scenes and costumes, indications of expression and action, and explanation of words and references not readily comprehensible.

The illustrations should aid immeasurably in visualizing the play. A description of the original staging, stage conditions, and stage techniques is provided partly as still another aid to visualization but principally to show how the playwright adapted his materials to suit the particular stage conventions of his time. Companioning each play are also a sketch of the author's life, an analysis of the play, and a selective bibliography to make this as much an all-in-one edition as possible.

Contents

The Playwright

I wish every night of my life,
like the first night at one of my plays.
— Farquhar

It is perhaps significant that Farquhar found his happiest moments chiefly in the world of the imagination. Other men would have preferred the more concrete pleasures of love fulfilled, of victory in politics or war. Had Farquhar lived in the early nineteenth century, he would have been a typical Utopian romantic, finding his felicity in the inner dream, the earth-transcending imagination. But he lived in a period too uncomplicated mentally and emotionally to furnish him with such a vision. Had he lived in Dreiser's America of the later nineteenth century, his life-role would have been similar to that of Carrie Meeber or Clyde Griffiths. He would have been the outsider, the sensitive and yearning, the diffident and ineffectual dreamer. He would have peered longingly through the wrought-iron gates, past the high walls and dark shade-trees into the luxurious life within doors — tempting but hidden and withdrawn. An early biographer says of him: "He was poor. His position was inferior. The irritating disproportion between the man he would wish to be and the man he was tended to make him socially diffident, clumsy of address . . ."

Farquhar desired life in abundance. But he was plagued with self-mistrust. His temperament aspired, only to find Fortune an intolerable coquette who lured but did not grant. Farquhar said of himself on one occasion, "Consider, I'm a man; a mortal, wishing, amorous

1

man." Yet he was enamored of a felicity that was perpetually to absent itself from his society. In another brief self-portrait, Farquhar said: "As to the mind, 'tis generally dressed like my person in black. Melancholy is its everyday apparel; and it has hitherto found few holidays to make it change its clothes." Hence in his comedies, he creates a *persona,* the glittering public personality that he would be, such as Archer in the present play, Roebuck of *Love and a Bottle,* and Sir Harry Wildair ("Still brisk and airy, I find, Sir Harry") of *The Constant Couple.* They are all men of unruffled and confident disposition, resourceful and radiant, undaunted. Quite unlike these invincible social conquerors, Farquhar reveals himself to us in a letter: "I went to the play this evening, and the music raised my soul to such a pitch of passion that I was almost mad for melancholy. I flew thence to Spring Garden, where with envious eyes I saw every man pick up his mate whilst I alone walked like solitary Adam . . . Thence I retired to the tavern where methought the shining glass represented your fair person." This is the tone of a reclusive man a little addicted to romantic nostalgia.

A good likeness of Farquhar appears in one of the early collected editions. It is a "presentation" scene in which Farquhar is being introduced to the Court of Apollo and the Nine Muses by faithful Ben Jonson. Farquhar's features are a trifle epicene, delicate and frail. The forehead is impressive, the brows well-defined, the eyes questioning and slightly reproachful. The mouth is the most expressive feature. It is drawn down into a pouting expression, marked with delicate lines of disillusionment. Not so strong as to be petulant, the expression is wistfully disappointed. It is the expression so often found in the characters of Dreiser's fictional world, the character whose "pain-touched mouth" is so indicative of "inexplicable longing." The delicate disillusionment etched in the expression is that of one who has followed and all but lost a fading vision. It suggests Caliban's awakening and longing to return to that sleep where "in dreaming,/The clouds methought would open, and show riches/Ready to drop upon me; that, when I waked,/I cried to dream again."

Of all of the writers of Restoration comedy from Etherege to Congreve and Vanbrugh, Farquhar, the last of the company, is, from the standpoint of worldly prosperity, the least of it. Of all of them, he is the one who is not the accepted gentleman of fashion and social position. Although he is the author of some of the most successful plays of his time, he seems to have dwelt always near the edge of need and neglect. Whatever his windfalls of fortune and dramatic triumph, they appear to have come to him as a perfumed breeze, delicious and gratifying, but fleeting, leaving him always as they had found him: with but the memory of good things, the hope of better. It is dramatically in keeping that his last and most successful play, *The Beaux' Stratagem,* was written on borrowed time, on borrowed money, and to some extent with materials borrowed from Vanbrugh, varied and flavored with a dash of Milton. To the end, he was a man somewhat alone and in need.

If there is a consistent theme or idea informing the entirety of Farquhar's writings, it is a satiric running commentary on the ugliness and degradation of poverty and praise for the grace of gold. There is a secondary emphasis on, and scorn for, the pretensions of "the gentleman," his outward pose and inner hollowness. "Murder and robbery!" cries the constable in *The Constant Couple;* "then he must be a gentleman." In the same play, Sir Harry Wildair scorns the imputation that he might be distressed if not taken for a gentleman. He disdains what he considers the false airs and superstition of being gentlemanly; instead he bestows his admiration on money. When presenting a purse of twenty guineas to a woman, he exclaims in lyrical rapture, "Why, then, madam, here is a nest of the prettiest goldfinches that ever chirped in a cage . . . twenty young ones . . . there is a great deal of wit and manners in twenty guineas." The same Sir Harry, perhaps Farquhar's favorite individual characterization, so reverences money that he proposes to a lady, without a trace of intended irony: "If the chastest, purest passion, with a large and fair estate, can make amends . . ." The serenity and peace that pass all understanding are themselves sustained by a substantial personal income: "A man of eight thousand pounds per annum be vexed! No, no; anger and spleen are companions for younger brothers." In his own self-portrait, Farquhar had said, "My character is very splenetic."

Conversely, if money was the "deity which all the world adores," scorn and derision fell upon those without it: "Tis one of the greatest curses of poverty to be the jest of chambermaids." Again, "Faugh, the nauseous fellow! He stinks of poverty already."

Doubtless, Farquhar's slightly obsessive preoccupation with money and gentility arose from his own feeling of estrangement from them. A lengthy *catena* of quotations bearing on these points could readily be compiled from his works. Farquhar had written illuminatingly in a letter about "keeping the springs of desire so long upon the rack" that "at last they grow loose and enervate." It was thus that in his life women, money, and social position teased and eluded him.

It would be tedious to pursue the issue further than the play before us. It contains the usual illustrations of Farquhar's preoccupation with such points. Mrs. Sullen reminds us that poets and philosophers have ever praised pastoral and rustic solitude because they lacked the money to enjoy the town. And the biological principle of "natural selection" is so subdued to that of artificial predilection in Aimwell that he tells us that "no woman can be a beauty without a fortune."

The spirit of Farquhar must have often visited Shaw as he wrote. Neither could resist the snapping of fingers under the noses of gentlemen. For example, Boniface of our play speaks of one who "is so much a gentleman every manner of way that he must be a highwayman." Shaw in *Man and Superman* presents John Tanner introducing himself: "I am a gentleman; I make my living by robbing the poor." When Shaw composed the Preface to *Major Barbara,* the spirit of Farquhar did not so much visit as dictate. "Undershaft, the hero of Major Barbara," Shaw writes, has "grasped the fact that poverty is a crime . . ." Then, more confidingly, Shaw adds, "What is new, as far as I know, is that article in Undershaft's religion which recognizes in Money the first need, and in poverty the vilest sin of man and society." Archer or Aimwell must have been the first begetters of the Undershaft strain, for it is they who made the sensational discovery mistakenly attributed by Shaw to Undershaft. Archer declares, "Don't mistake me, Aimwell, for 'tis my maxim that there is no scandal like rags nor any crime so shameful as poverty." To which Aimwell replies, "The world confesses it every day in its practice, though men won't own it for their opinion." The Beaux then go on to discuss "poor Jack Generous" (suspiciously like the poor, cast-off Peter Shirley of *Major Barbara*). Aimwell asks, "But did you observe poor Jack Generous in the park last week?" Archer responds, "Yes . . . melancholly face . . . picking his useless teeth . . . single and solitary as a lion in a desert." Thereupon Aimwell turns again to the Undershaft discovery, as though Farquhar could not let so grave a matter rest with a single notice: "And as much avoided, for no crime upon earth but the want of money." It is needless to remark that with Farquhar poverty was the crime of the individual, not of society.

Poverty walked with Farquhar to the end of the lane. Ill, penniless, and miserable, lodged in a back garret in

St. Martin's Lane, London, he was given timely relief by his life-long friend, the popular actor Robert Wilks. Despite Farquhar's desolation and penury, Wilks urged him to write another comedy for relief of himself and his family. "Come, George, banish melancholy, draw your drama, and I will call on you this day week to see it; but as an empty pocket may cramp your genius, I desire you will accept of my mite." Wilks gave him twenty guineas. Was Wilks thinking (he was a triumph in the role of Sir Harry Wildair) of the twenty chirping goldfinches? Farquhar was right in saying that there was much wit in twenty guineas. Presumably they made a great contribution to *The Beaux' Stratagem*.

Of this last heroic effort of a constitution always frail, we are told in an account traceable to Wilks: ". . . the most part of it he wrote in his bed, and before he had finished the second act, he perceived the approaches of death." The exact moment of the premonitory vision of the end is doubtless legendary. But that Farquhar wrote what is probably his best comedy on his death-bed is reasonably well established. The fact has vastly overstimulated ambitious biographers. Reveling in the mood of *La Boheme,* they have elicited the last sigh of pathos for struggling genius expiring in picturesque squalor. In thus wringing delight from bitterest hours, Farquhar must have satisfied the feelings of a Yeats. Wilde could have asked for nothing more. When did man ever more fully demonstrate the triumph of art over life? Farquhar's last-hour accomplishment is a reversal of Thomas Mann's familiar contest between the declining artist and all-triumphant "life," as in *Tristan* or *Death in Venice*.

Farquhar was not of the romantic era. Death in St. Martin's Lane, London, in 1707 found him neither splendidly disintegrating in romantic despair nor heavily dejected. He mournfully mentions his condition in both the "Advertisement" of his play and the "Epilogue." But that is all. If he was far from finding all of life like the first night of a new play, he at least made death wait outside the door until he completed the final draft of a new play. The eternal Footman did not snicker as he held Farquhar's coat. The comedy was launched, crackling with laughter and triumph, before Farquhar's departure. Whatever his frailties and follies, he behaved at the end as a Shakespearean hero, most eloquent in death. His own merriment outmocked that of "the merry worm that wakes beneath."

However gay and happy the Beaux and their stratagems may be, one is none the less made to feel the delicately elegiac undercurrent, the tender nostalgia for life that touches the comedy here and there. There is, for instance, in Archer's reference to London a slightly equivocal note, more strongly nostalgic than one might expect in the situation: ". . . so much Pleasure for so much Money, we have had our Pennyworths, and had I Millions, I wou'd go to the same Market again. O London, London! . . . Past Pleasures, for ought I know are best . . . those to come may disappoint us." The nostalgic modulates into the elegiac as Mrs. Sullen plaintively meditates: "Love and Death have their Fatalities, and strike home one time or other: — You'll pay for all one Day, I warrant ye." To have the bill presented at the age of twenty-nine was a trifle hard.

In keeping with the life of one who clung so precariously to the fringes of fortune's garment, Farquhar's biography is scanty and where most interesting, as in his pursuit of elusive and shadowy females, most speculative. The life-design of ambition without fulfillment is set early. Indeed the motives of Farquhar's life were in a way those of Kite of *The Recruiting Officer*. When asked why he entered the service, he replied, "Hunger and ambition."

Farquhar was born in the North of Ireland in 1677. He came of one of those families which having begotten a man of talent is thereafter referred to as needy but "good." Farquhar was lucky enough to receive good early training in Latin and Greek at Derry, where he fell under the influence of Ellis Walker, a former scholar of Trinity College, Dublin. From Derry Farquhar also found his way to Trinity College. He matriculated in July of 1694 and entered a *sizar*, a collegiate status considered then both inferior and menial. Early in 1695 Farquhar had improved his situation slightly by becoming Exhibitioner at £4 a year.

He did not, however, long enjoy the new advantage, limited as it was. Among a number of students disciplined for disorderly behavior at a Fair in the outskirts of Dublin, Farquhar was one. Although later reinstated in his Exhibition, Farquhar did not long remain at Trinity. According to tradition, Farquhar had already made himself unpopular with the College authorities by including in an essay profanely facetious remarks upon New Testament miracles. At any rate, his name does not apear upon the College register after February of 1696. Farquhar left without a degree, apparently to take temporary employment as a proofreader in the printing shop of an acquaintance of his brother.

During the winter of 1695-96, Smock Alley, the theatrical area of Dublin, had attracted the attention of Farquhar. *Hamlet* and the players had become his main interest, not the University. Farquhar's later references in his plays to the "University men" are not complimentary. When he describes Sir Harry Wildair, the character he would himself have perhaps most wished to be, the former is described as a "gentleman of the most happy circumstances, born to a plentiful estate." But one of his special privileges was that he was given a "genteel and easy education free from the rigidness of teachers and the pedantry of schools." In the same play with Sir Harry is a Lady Lurewell who speaks of two collegians who "had a heavy, pedantic, university air, a sort of disagreeable scholastic boorishness in their behavior." Farquhar's disciplinary superiors had been paid off.

He found luck in Smock Alley in the early part of 1696. Ashbury, the manager of a theatre, was happy to have a University man among his actors. He was a generous manager and set the young scholar up in business. It was then also that Farquhar had the good fortune to make a life-long friend of Robert Wilks, already an actor of note and somewhat older than Farquhar. Although assigned at once demanding roles in Ashbury's productions, Farquhar was not well equipped either mentally or physically as an actor. He was never to become what he admired in his creation Sir Harry Wildair: "The joy of the playhouse, the life of the Park," one "whose florid constitution never ruffled . . . turning all passion into gaiety of humour . . ." Rather, Farquhar is described as being of frail constitution and delicate temperamental balance. Characteristically, a little too much wine usually gave him a morning's remorse far exceeding the evening's tepid riot.

A contemporary tradition passing from Wilks to Cibber describes Farquhar as being of "proper gesture and just elocution" but "unhappy in voice . . . not power enough . . . defective in point of assurance, nor could ever overcome his natural timidity." Ashbury, then, was over-zealous and more than hopeful in casting Farquhar in the role of Othello as his initial stage effort. If ever a role required what Farquhar did not have it is that of Othello — physical robustness, sonorous voice, imposing presence. Farquhar's thin voice and meagre countenance, shy manner and uncertain temperament must have reduced Othello to something of the stature of Roderigo. More judicious casting followed as the year 1696 wore on: the role of Lennox in *Macbeth,* that of Bellair in *The Man of Mode.*

Early in 1697 Farquhar was playing the part of Guyomar in Dryden's *Indian Emperor, or The Conquest of*

Mexico. Farquhar quite excusably suffered an absence of mind near the end of one of those grandiloquent passages of quite unheroic "heroic" verse in which, as Johnson tartly noted, passion slept while declamation roared. Farquhar failed to exchange a sword for a foil. As a result, he seriously wounded his fellow actor Price. But the moral shock was mightier than the incision. It was Price who recovered. Farquhar did not. The incident impelled Farquhar to give up acting. Probably the accident precipitated doubts and uncertainties already at work.

Again Fortune, having tripped him, picked him up. Ashbury, the manager, with quite unusual kindness, gave Farquhar a "benefit" night to signalize his premature retirement as an actor — even to the relinquishing of the "house charges," which Ashbury might reasonably have kept to defray management expenses. Robert Wilks, Farquhar's guiding angel (he was about twelve years older), directed his steps to London. Farquhar later arranged to have Wilks brought to London. Like Alpinists they helped each other up the slope. Wilks added his own contribution of £10 to the £50 which Ashbury's goodness had provided. In 1697 Farquhar touched English soil, a fact commemorated two and a half centuries later in 1947 by the special revival of *The Beaux' Stratagem* in Manchester. Two years later there was a second brilliant revival in London at the Phoenix Theatre.

Farquhar disappears from our view for a time. One wonders whether the reminiscences of squalid poverty occurring in the conversation of Archer and Aimwell date their origin from this probably difficult interval. As for the London stage, Vanbrugh was the reigning dramatist at the hour of Farquhar's arrival. *The Relapse,* given in 1696, was fading into grateful memory. In 1697 *The Provok'd Wife* was playing to enthusiastic audiences. Since it was part of Farquhar's plan in invading England to try his hand at writing for the stage, he must have observed Brother Van's work with absorbed curiosity. Certainly he did not forget it. For when he composed his own last play, *The Beaux' Stratagem*, he may, in main incidents and plot-design, have drawn upon these two plays. The Archer-Sullen bedroom scene, which still shocked our Victorian forbears as "almost voluptuous," was in imitation of a slightly more virile scene in *The Relapse*. The further resemblance of Squire and Mrs. Sullen to Vanbrugh's Sir John and Lady Brute we shall consider later.

The two most endearing occupations, the two most interesting words to the London beaux of the day were employed in the title of Farquhar's first play: *Love and a Bottle*. Were Farquhar alive today, we would accuse him of having consulted a public relations expert about the wording of a title. In the play, George Roebuck, the first of his irrepressible and irresponsible adventurers, caught the fancy of the London audiences. The play appeared successfully at Drury Lane in December, 1698. It was at the end of the same year in which Collier had launched his thunderbolt at the Restoration stage. The play bore little evidence of having been influenced by that clergyman's torrid assault, although later comedies were to reflect the influence.

From this point on, Farquhar's career moves along an uncertain, tortuous pathway. There are successes and failures in love and drama. From the little that we can gather, the love pursuit appears to have been as laughable but much less lively than the plays. In his biography *Young George*, Mr. Willard Connely traces the numerous somewhat shadowy and feckless "affairs" in which Farquhar was involved — the random, now hot, now cold mode of pursuit. Mr. Connely has told the story, such as it is, better than others.

In 1699 Farquhar published the *Adventures of Covent Garden*. It was inspired by the *City Romance*, the Eng-

lish title of Furetière's original *Roman Bourgeoise*. Farquhar's work was a mixture of observed London life
and private fantasy. Elements of plot and character he
later used dramatically. Towards the end of this same
year, Farquhar had his really grand slam success: *The
Constant Couple,* dominated by the already mentioned
Sir Harry Wildair. "Never did anything such wonders"
is a typical admiring comment. Early in 1701 Farquhar
attempted a sequel to *The Constant Couple.* But *Sir
Harry Wildair,* the sequel, conceded too much to the
new moral climate brought in with Jeremy Collier's
Short View. It failed to win the success of its predecessor. In 1702, after returning from Holland, Farquhar
brought out *The Inconstant,* an adaptation of Fletcher's
Wild-Goose Chase. At the end of the same year, Farquhar's *The Twin Rivals* also appeared.

We now come to the period in Farquhar's dramatic
career which his biographers call "the gap." For approx-
imately four years, Farquhar did not write another comedy. Then suddenly in 1706 and 1707, he flashes into
view like a dolphin sporting in the sunset. In 1706 *The
Recruiting Officer* had a lively reception. Early in 1707
The Beaux' Stratagem likewise delighted applauding
audiences. After that, the silence.

In 1702 Farquhar, apparently catching at any little
profit that might be in the trade winds, published a
curious miscellany of "Occasionary Verse and Epistola-
tory Prose" under the title of *Love and Business.* The
governing principle of the selection was evidently based
upon a superstitious veneration for "variety." In the
collection were odds and ends of youthful *jeux d'esprit*
surviving from his undergraduate days, amorous poems,
a song or two, some epigrams. Included also were quite
recent specimens of seductive letters to susceptible ladies giving more than hints of Farquhar's own London
adventures and escapades with his "Penelope," his
"Chloe," etc.

Biographically more significant was the verbal self-portrait sent to an admirer in place of a requested drawing. Calling it "The Picture," Farquhar insisted that it gave a better likeness than a Van Dyke or a Kneller could have done. The little composition picturesquely outlined the temperament and plight of "the intellectual" of all times, prophetically reaching even to Trofimof of *The Cherry Orchard*. Farquhar summed up the type by noting that his worldly "estate" had boundaries defined by the circumference of his hat. To complete the medley, Farquhar tossed in a *Discourse upon Comedy*. In the latter, his prophetic touch came nearer home. Of drama and its makers: "Naked she came into the world, and 'tis to be feared, like its professors, will go naked out." The volume reflects Farquhar's reckless eclectic bent in all things but reminds us that it was not until the last two comedies that he had perfected the harmonizing talent that enabled him to fuse mutually alien or unsympathetic elements into family unity.

Published just before "the gap," *Love and Business* calls to mind that the title of Farquhar's first play was *Love and a Bottle*. The titles register a change. Love has become associated not with diversion and recreation but with economic activity. Perhaps the latter title reflects Farquhar's subconscious preoccupation: a calm, cool scrutinizing of the social horizon for a wife who was also an heiress. Whether it does or not, Farquhar early in 1703 married Mrs. Margaret Pemell, widow of an Army officer. That she was some ten years older than Farquhar is not especially significant since he appeared to find solace, both physical and spiritual, in the company of ladies somewhat older. But Mrs. Pemell's ten-year advantage had not been without incident. She brought with her to the marriage three children, two of them dependent, both girls. On the basis of scanty evidence, contemporaries and subsequent biographers

speculated as to why the nearly always indigent Farquhar should have at last dropped anchor on such a
bleak and wind-swept shore.

The traditional explanation almost uniformly accepted is that Mrs. Pemell, contributing in persistence
what she lacked in prettiness, was a pursuing woman
in the high manner of Ann Whitefield, Shaw's Every-
woman. Fascinated by the wayward Farquhar as a man
of affairs and a dramatist of reputation, Mrs. Pemell is
supposed to have falsely represented herself as an heiress of £700 a year. Other accounts evade such definite
statement but agree to the imposture as a last desperate
maneuver to lure the reluctant Farquhar into marriage.
It explains the fact of his marrying an infatuated older
woman with two dependents when Farquhar had dem-
onstrated that he was scarcely able to support himself.

Farquhar himself without doubt shared the attitude
of his Beaux and of early medieval artists: women and
saints look their prettiest silhouetted against a patina
of bright gold. Unfortunately, Farquhar's Margaret did
not bring any redeeming portion of this world to a man
who was in voluptuous possession of his own soul. Actually or almost penniless, she brought to Farquhar increased responsibility. Here again in another aspect of
his career was the same kind of *gaucherie,* the same sort
of grotesque mistake that had marked his earlier entry
into the world of acting. This time fortune stabbed
Farquhar.

Yet despite the ambition of biographers and critics
who would find in *The Beaux' Stratagem* an attack on
strict divorce laws arising from Farquhar's own misad-
venture, Farquhar's contemporaries and successors have
preserved a tradition quite otherwise. A Memoir in an
early edition of Farquhar's plays reflects, if not an as-
certained fact, certainly the accepted belief about the
marriage: "To his honour be it spoken, though he
found himself deceived, and his circumstances embar-

rassed, yet he never once upbraided her for the cheat, but behaved to her with all the delicacy and tenderness of an indulgent husband." Not only was there an external harmony; the tradition also reports an interior, spiritual harmony, quite the opposite to that obtaining between the married couple of *The Beaux' Stratagem.* Of Farquhar, his friends said that he was "so charmed with her love and understanding that he entirely forgave her, and liv'd very happily with her." Whatever the truth of the matter, one thing is clear. The immediate tradition concerning Farquhar is that he did *not* use the comedy as an expression of his own matrimonial disaffection.

Perhaps, then, the marriage of 1703 explains sufficienty why, until 1706, Farquhar's muse, jealous and exasperated, abandoned him. In 1704 Farquhar appears to us in his character as Lieutenant of the Grenadiers, commissioned by the Duke of Ormonde, Lord-Lieutenant of Ireland. Actually, the lieutenancy was worth to him a little better than £54 a year. Neither marital nor martial connection supplied him with munificence. At any rate, his military duties took him out of London and into the provinces. The move was not without significance to English comedy, for it too was taken on the road. Thereafter Farquhar's plots had a setting outside of London and in the country: *The Recruiting Officer* was set in Shrewsbury; *The Beaux' Stratagem* in Lichfield. Henceforth mingled with London beaux are squires, country gentry and dowagers, rural landlords, and provincial country servants. Young Marlowe is already being introduced to Tony Lumpkin and Diggory.

The Play

It would be heretical to approach Farquhar, especially his reputation as the author of *The Recruiting Officer* and *The Beaux' Stratagem,* without invoking the word *transitional.* Or better, some conventional metaphor to the effect that Farquhar's plays are a series of locks through which the comic drama of the Restoration — the high, dry, witty sex-intrigue of Etherege, Wycherley, and Congreve — is lowered to the depressed, marshy levels of the New or Sentimental Comedy of Steele and Cibber, Kelley and Cumberland. Also it would be justifiable to look back upon Farquhar nostalgically as the last, exotic bloom in the sunset garden of Restoration comedy. Or looking ahead less sentimentally, we might simply regard him as the first among the dramatists to be considered in a survey of *Eighteenth Century Drama,* as does Mr. Frederick S. Boas in his volume of that title.

In a larger perspective, the historian might contemplate Farquhar as a literary Noah, appearing on the scene immediately after the fierce denunciations of the righteous and wrathful prophet Collier in his *Short View of the Immorality and Profaneness of the English Stage* (1698). The first heavy drops of the *Comédie larmoyante* begin to fall. Farquhar's last plays become the ark in which are stored the comic materials later to be salvaged. When the flood-waters of the New comedy receded finally and the ark had grounded itself on the sunny beach of the 1770's, Goldsmith found therein much of the material needed for his anti-Sentimental comedy *She Stoops to Conquer.* A close comparison of Goldsmith's play with Farquhar's *Beaux' Stratagem* will disclose remarkable parallels of plot and dialogue, descending even to minute details of wording. Indeed, so happy was Goldsmith with what he discovered in the ark that he borrowed what Farquhar promised but neglected to perform. For example, Farquhar's *Dramatis Personae* informs us that Lady Bountiful was "foolishly fond of her Son Sullen." The characterization gives little or no indication of the fact. But Goldsmith loyally took over the suggestion, and old Mrs. Hardcastle becomes the doting, daft mother of young Squire Lumpkin. The latter is half-brother to the lively Kate as Farquhar's Squire Sullen is half-brother to the amiable Dorinda.

It is clear that Farquhar, both as a personality and as a writer, is a fairly complex figure. *Transitional,* at any rate, is too ambiguous a label to affix to the diverse ingredients that make up *The Beaux' Stratagem.* Certainly the play is a *pot pourri,* an *olla podrida,* a versatile blending of a diversity of comic principle, character, and event — in whatever language we may choose to describe Farquhar's masterful harmonizing skill. We might say of him what Shaw said of Wilde in the mid-nineties: "our only thorough playwright. He plays with everything: with wit, with philosophy, with drama . . ."

Farquhar gives us the comedy of wit in his city beaux who seek their quarry indifferently in Church and boudoir; the comedy of humors in his broadly sketched and strongly marked country gentry and dowagers; sex intrigue and sentiment, satire and edification, the realistic treatment of a decomposing marriage and the sentimental handling of a new romance. Farquhar's harmonizing ingenuity and plot inventiveness enable him to construct a dramatic harness so that he can drive with ease animals of different temper and species as a single team. His distinguishing and distinguished skill is that he moulds into unity strangely diverse materials.

In this harlequin variety, we encounter fantastical

French officers and Irish pretenders who mix a brogue with a continental accent. We meet country servants like Scrub who quote Latin neatly and patly only to confuse ideas in English delightfully. A landlord of a country inn admires spoken Latin and judges of its excellence by the rapidity of its articulation. We encounter the most urbane of highwaymen, one as conscious of ecclesiastical rights (and rites) as we are of civil: to this highwayman (Gibbet) facing death: "Come rogue, if you have a short Prayer, say it," Gibbet pertly answering: "Sir, I have no prayer at all; the Government has provided a Chaplain to say Prayers for us on these occasions." It is the manner of General Burgoyne in Shaw's *The Devil's Disciple,* addressing himself to the condemned Dick Dudgeon. Poverty and physical ailment are made light of with equal facility. Mrs. Sullen's monstrous prescription for curing an ailing leg darkly resembles Swift's *A Modest Proposal* in its ironically ruthless tone. We have already noted Shaw's borrowing of witticisms on poverty.

Archer is himself a triumph of the variety of tactic. When Squire Sullen naturally declines to "deliver" over his own wife to her would-be seducer, Archer with superb, mocking insolence inquires: "What do's the Man mean? not part with his Wife?" Midnight burglars are routed and supplanted by chivalrous protectors who immediately attempt bedroom seduction as their prerogative and reward. Archer protects Mrs. Sullen but after apprehending her assailant, he demands of her: "Here, Madam, lend me your Garter?" His resourcefulness in improvising manacles and his effrontery in making advances to the defended lady leave even Mrs. Sullen bewildered. She cannot be sure whether she is another Eve being lured by the serpent of old Eden or merely the next victim of the common variety of garter-snake. In a single scene Farquhar mingles the most outrageous farce and the wittiest sex-intrigue. His dazzling variety of invention, contained ingeniously within a single plot, is unconsciously described by Mrs. Sullen's comment on her rescuer Archer: "The Devil's in this Fellow; he fights, loves, and banters, all in a Breath."

It is a heady mixture but given a measure of unity by one dominant mode of comic treatment. Farquhar consistently uses the device of anti-climax, the interrupted quest or aborted adventure. Perhaps it was a projected mode of his own experience of life.

Archer, for instance, is promptly intercepted in his designs upon the piquant Cherry by the unscheduled appearance of the father Boniface. Next Count Bellair is lured by Mrs. Sullen. She has "planted" her unwary husband within hearing distance as she invites the advances of the Count in the hope that the husband will discover an aphrodisiac exhilaration in finding his rejected and neglected wife tempting to other men. Hence Count Bellair is interrupted at the critical moment by an irate husband with drawn sword who is himself unexpectedly confronted with a wife with "presented" pistol. Count Bellair, in a mood of amorous revenge, plans to have himself secreted in Mrs. Sullen's bedroom, where at the psychological he hopes to capture the biological moment at last. He is unknowingly anticipated and superseded in this dubious ambush by Archer, who having heard of the stratagem by means of a bribe, substitutes himself as the hidden philanderer. Then, he too is deprived of his questionable advantage by the cry and then the presence of thieves, who themselves encounter disappointment by finding that they have chosen the wrong moment: they are thwarted and captured by Archer with the help of Aimwell. Archer has already set out upon his quest of Mrs. Sullen in a mood of jingo patriotism, fashionable at the moment:

For where a French-man durst attempt to storm
A Briton sure may well the Work perform.

He now attempts to exploit his advantage as "protector" of Mrs. Sullen. He, too, is now thwarted by the unexpected arrival of Sir Charles Freeman, brother of the amorously yearning but retreating Mrs. Sullen. In this series of contretemps, almost every variety of male relative contributes to the anticlimax: father, husband, and brother.

Farquhar's wit has affinities with both that of Wilde and Shaw, yet it is basically different. Shaw's is the rational, intellectual wit exploring the pathology of the social tissue. Wilde's is the mental costume of the dandy, the finely tailored epigram. Farquhar's wit is more varied and ample but less precisely aimed or formulated. It is the wit of the alert, ironic, yet wondering observer contemplating with inner amazement the absurdity of things, yet without any formula for renovation or any posture of cynical detachment.

The Beaux' Stratagem as a comedy of wit and sex intrigue presents Aimwell, younger and impecunious brother of a Lord, and Archer, his resourceful and needy companion. Their alternating role of man and servant, both in search of a beautiful heiress, is a plot sufficiently appealing that Mr. P. G. Wodehouse reissued it in his novel *French Leave,* in which masquerading ladies are substituted for men in pursuit of romance and fortune. In Farquhar's plot, at the outset both are philanderers and amorists, adventurers and fortune-hunters descending upon the provinces in search of their pleasing heiress. They are men of fashion, given to love and drink, formerly of some affluence but now of exhausted fortune. With regret and half-bemused nostalgia, they recollect vanished happiness.

The complications attendant upon their quest introduce a growing differentiation in character. Although in Archer the Restoration beau is preserved for the most part, Aimwell undergoes a romantic and edifying change of heart. Conscience transforms the predatory rake of

Restoration tradition into the sentimental hero of the
New or Sentimental comedy: a man suddenly given to
virtuous idealism born of the unexpected influence of
virtuous female beauty. Hence we have preserved in
Archer the older tradition of satire and realism; in Aimwell we look forward to the Sentimental comedy of edification and propriety, discreetly attended by substantial
financial success.

In characterization Archer and Aimwell are like two
rivulets which, beginning from the same hill-top, diverge
increasingly as they move along their forward journey.
Both begin as philandering, fortune-hunting adventurers. Unlike Archer, Aimwell is transformed by female
beauty of character as well as person. He undergoes a
radical moral conversion and shifts to the side of the
angels. Farquhar, stretching to the limit his desire for
diversity, thus combines in one comedy those elements
kept separate by his Restoration predecessors: sex and
marriage, love and loyalty, amorous delight and domes-
ticity. This divergence of Aimwell from Archer is suit-
ably expressed at the end of the comedy in a rather
Shavian predicament. Aimwell, still under his original
obligation to Archer to divide any booty resulting from
their expedition, presents the latter with a dramatic
choice between Dorinda (the fair lady) and the fair
lady's fortune. The offer is not belittling to Dorinda
since the now regenerated Aimwell knows that the old
unrepentant sinner Archer will take the cash and let
the moral credit go.

Then in the almost inevitable manner of what eventually came to be the New or Sentimental comedy,
Aimwell's brother dies. He has been living offstage in
apparently flourishing health but evidently with an exquisite sense of time and occasion. By means of his sudden death, Farquhar promptly subsidizes morality with
the title and fortune to which the hitherto unredeemed
Aimwell had been merely the idle pretender. The union

of material reward and moral endeavor was already present. The cash-nexus between honor and its consequences was eventually to taint with suspicion the morality of the Sentimental comedy. From the start, however, the heirs to the kingdom of heaven approached their reward in a coach and six. The equivocal nature of this spirit of reform in the Sentimental hero is evident not merely in the grandiose rhetoric of regeneration but likewise in subsequent reflections upon it.

Aimwell's sudden moral rebirth is presented in his reflections upon the virtuous nature of the beautiful lady he is about to deceive: "Such goodness who cou'd injure; I find myself unequal to the task of Villain; she has gain'd my Soul, and made it honest like her own . . . judge of my Passion by my Conversion." Only slightly later he confides to Archer: ". . . methought she receiv'd my Confession with Pleasure." Noble sentiment is promptly blessed by the god of expedience. Presently, Dorinda enters — in obedience to stage directions "mighty gay." And rightly so. For she brings news of Aimwell's succession to title and fortune to which she adds her own readiness to forgive and enjoy. Not only does good fortune ensue readily upon Aimwell's apparent renunciation of base impulse, but he has in a way obscurely anticipated the practical benefit of higher ones.

Aimwell's change from predatory rake to man of moral probity and high feeling is underlined in that his spiritual rebirth takes place at a crucial moment in the rake's progress. He is simultaneously implicated in two of the standard devices of seduction resorted to by Restoration stage-rakes on the make for money: 1) the "clandestine" and 2) the "tricked" marriage.

As to the first, Aimwell plans to marry Dorinda outside of canonical hours. Foigard is to officiate although he is not a priest of the Anglican succession nor an authorized representative of the Church. Secondly, Aimwell has falsely presented himself in name, title, and fortune. Hence his sudden renunciation of his lower self marks the rejection of a well-defined practice of the Restoration rake. Despite this sudden display of exquisite feeling, Aimwell is curiously insensitive to the loss of a brother, whose name and memory he had so nearly betrayed. His dry crust of repentance and severely controlled brotherly sorrow are transformed easily into the manna of jubilation. He might have been perfectly at home in *The Importance of Being Earnest*, except for the gravely limiting factor that he *was* in earnest.

Aimwell thus stands near the beginning of what is to be the grand succession of the Sentimental hero as he appears first in stage and eventually in fictional tradition. The shadows of Tom Jones, Charles Surface, Young Marlowe, etc. are already cast upon the screen of the future. All are typical of those dashing young rips of easy morals whose tarnished souls are miraculously brightened and made radiant by contact with exquisite female goodness enshrined in beauty of person — yet not without a favorable cash balance. The kind of love relationship in which this tradition ultimately culminated is expressed with subtly humorous grace by Lord David Cecil: ". . . a tender sentiment for a virtuous object, founded largely on esteem, precious for its power to elevate life and sweeten character but always under the ultimate control of reason and virtue." It is perhaps significant that Farquhar has Dorinda fall in love with Aimwell at Church service.

Archer as a representative of the older comic tradition of satire and realism is quite otherwise. In Farquhar's first play *Love and a Bottle*, a hero of comedy is described as being among other things: "A Compound of practical Rake, and speculative Gentleman, who always bears off the great Fortune in the Play." It suits Archer. As amorist and fortune-seeker, Archer has a touch of the picaresque rogue as well as that of the Restoration rake. Like the latter he pursues the pleasures of drink, play, and love. But like the rogue, he is the resourceful and witty rascal who is totally indifferent to the well-being of others when his own interests are at stake. He warns perpetually against committing matrimony without benefit of a substantial dowry. He is also a man of quixotic pride, rejecting the pert and winsome Cherry not only because of her insufficient dowry but because she is a servant. Crossing moral boundaries does not trouble him, but class lines are sacred. Besides acquiring money, his one ambition is to treat all attractive females as Alexander Pope accused Mrs. Aphra Behn of doing with her stage characters. Referring to her as Astrea, Pope wrote:

> The stage how loosely does Astrea tread
> Who fairly puts all characters to bed.

For all of that, Archer is more than a thoughtless irresponsible child of laughter and delight. He is a philosophical and rational rake: "Give me a man that keeps his five senses keen and bright as his sword; . . . detaches 'em by turns upon whatever party of pleasure agreeably offers . . . I can stick to my bottle while my wine, my company, and my reason, holds good; I can be charmed with Sappho's singing without falling in love with her face . . . I love a fine house, but let another keep it; and just so I love a fine woman."

Archer's statement might stand as the obituary of the Restoration rake who retired before the chilling blasts of Jeremy Collier in 1698. By 1707 the moral climate had so altered that Archer's manifesto is almost "reactionary." Indeed, the icy touch of Collier is not absent from Archer's career. Despite his reckless pursuit of Cherry and Mrs. Sullen, he remains at the final curtain desirous of both but having enjoyed neither. Indeed, Archer's most human, if not his most edifying or most characteristic expression, is his cry: "Rot the money; I've lost my wench."

Yet it was money that Archer sought primarily, despite moments of transient weakness. Farquhar's immediate predecessor Vanbrugh wrote for one of his characters a line often quoted as both symptomatic and prophetic of the change in the *ethos* of the Restoration hero and stage: ". . . to be capable of loving one, doubtless is better than to possess a Thousand." Archer doubtless felt that it was much preferable to possess a Thousand, provided they be pounds, and thereby be free to love many.

In character he is a mixture of Shakespeare's Mercutio and Shaw's Captain Bluntschli of *Arms and the Man*. Like Mercutio, he thinks of love as a game and a sport, not to be taken seriously. Hence Archer keeps alive the light-hearted, frivolous attitude toward love of the older stage tradition, the tradition that went underground during the Sentimental period to reappear so brilliantly in *The Importance of Being Earnest*. The somewhat artificially introduced "catechism of love" by Archer and Cherry preserves this spirit. In his encounter with Cherry as with Mrs. Sullen, Archer's wit and high-spirited gaiety are in contrast with the fulsome rhetoric of the sober-hearted lover, the sentimental-sublime that characterizes so many of the exchanges between Dorinda and Aimwell.

Like Captain Bluntschli, but without his Olympian competence, Archer possesses a whimsically realistic and anti-romantic wit. In the bedroom scene, having been the valiant protector of Mrs. Sullen's virtue, Archer turns arch-seducer and demands favors for services rendered. To considerations of gallantry and chivalry placed before him as an impediment, he retorts: "Look 'ye, Madam, I'm none of your Romantick Fools, that fight Gyants and Monsters for nothing; my Valour is down right Swiss; I'm a Soldier of Fortune and must be paid." We might be listening to a Restoration Chocolate Soldier chiding his Raina for offering only chocolates.

Dorinda and Mrs. Sullen, the female opposites to Aimwell and Archer, are like their male counterparts a contrast: the idealistic and edifying set off against the realistic and sardonic. But with this difference. Mrs. Sullen more than any of the other characters in the play is an individualized, complex human being who cannot be easily labelled.

Mrs. Sullen is a sophisticated lady of fashion and pleasure transplanted from London to a provincial town. Her pointed and invidious comparisons do not allow us to forget the social distance she has travelled. Dorinda of the four is the only representative of the country gentry. Besides being a "feeder" of lines to Mrs. Sullen, allowing the latter to voice her marital distress and desolation, Dorinda is an attractively fresh and convincing character in her own right. Although idealized, she is not merely the virtuously self-conscious, demurely proper, moralizing heroine who reclaims wild and wayward young men for the more tame satisfactions of domestic society. There is much in her lively spirit that is a foreshadowing of Goldsmith's Kate Hardcastle.

When we first see Dorinda, she is uneasy about Mrs. Sullen's possibly straying into intimacy with visiting male charmers. But after falling in love herself with Aimwell, Dorinda acknowledges an increased susceptibility to the elemental attraction of sex. She does not hesitate to say that she no longer finds it unnatural to actively contemplate man as a bedfellow: ". . . while the Mind is conversant with Flesh and Blood, it must conform to the Humours of the Company," she puts it whimsically. The remark elicits from Mrs. Sullen one of her most human comments: "How a little Love and good Company improves a Woman." Far from being merely a frigid advocate of the sobering qualities of chaste love, Dorinda is quite susceptible to a little lush flattery: "My Lord has told me that I have more Wit and Beauty than any of my Sex; and truly I begin to think the Man is sincere." Perhaps the most sprightly expression of Dorinda's charm and animation is her rapturous vision of the anticipated delights of marriage: ". . . the Park, the Play, and the drawing-Room, Splendour, Equipage, Noise and Flambeaux — Hey — my Lady Aimwell's Servants there — Lights, Lights to the Stairs — My Lady Aimwell's Coach put forward — Stand by, make room for her Ladyship —" The country girl's dream of the Town.

If Farquhar's portrait of Dorinda is that of a delightful young lady brought painlessly to the threshold of felicity, his characterization of Mrs. Sullen is less simple. Obviously we are conscious of her at first as the wife of Squire Sullen. As such, Mrs. Sullen's mode of existence is variously described in metaphors ranging from war to animal husbandry. She tells Count Bellair that she is a "Prisoner of War" and in the best battle-of-the-sexes tradition comments that in marriage "a Woman must wear chains." Mrs. Sullen dejectedly asks of Dorinda: "And must the fair Apartment of my Breast be made a Stable for a Brute to lie in?"

The quality of the "Brute," her husband the Squire, was adequately expressed in another context when Mrs. Sullen was contemplating the world of instinct and feeling in relation to the rigidity of law: "What Law can search into the remote Abyss of Nature?" The phrase unwittingly descriptive of her husband is "Abyss of Nature." He has not even the redeeming trait of being remote. The chasm of his deficiency, his yawning emptiness, presents every impediment not merely to the marriage of true minds but even of amiable mindlessness.

In herself Mrs. Sullen is a character of varying

whims, moods, sentiments, and urges. She is not the traditional female rake of Restoration comedy to be found, for example in *The Country Wife* or *The Way of the World*. She tends that way by inclination, but the impulsion is checked by scruple. In comparing her existence to that of a prisoner of war, she adds that she is restrained likewise from freedom of decision by "Parole of Honour." Nor is she the ordinary, bored London-bred wife of a sottish country squire. Her boredom gives rise at times to a distinctly prickly bitterness, one at times sadistic enough to satisfy even Hedda Gabler. But along with this bitterness, softening and humanizing it, is a wistful quality, a languorous pessimism and melancholy that arouse rather than alienate our sympathy. It is the interplay of these qualities of mind that makes Mrs. Sullen hardly a comic character, for Farquhar is evidently too much in sympathy with her to preserve the detachment necessary for laughter.

Mrs. Sullen's sense of helplessness is complicated by a strain of irony. Early in the play, she says to Dorinda that she is ready to go to Church: "Anywhere to Pray; for Heaven alone can help me . . ." Quickly she spices her sadness with the astringent afterthought: "But, I think, Dorinda, there's no Form of Prayer in the Liturgy against bad Husbands." At the same moment, Mrs. Sullen, despite her own desolation of spirit can take a sympathetic view of Dorinda's inexperience in regard to love, saying: "You like nothing, your time is not come; Love and Death have their Fatalities, and strike home one time or other." It is a line that might have been spoken by the tragic Duchess of Malfi. At other times, her reflective melancholy modulates into a Keatsian pathos, something vaguely reminiscent of the gentle despair of the *Ode to a Nightingale*. After Dorinda's hour of romance has arrived and she is rapturously imagining the pleasures of married life with

Aimwell, Mrs. Sullen exclaims: "Happy, happy Sister! your Angel has been watchful for your Happiness, whilst mine has slept regardless of his Charge. — Long smiling Years of circling Joys for you, but not one Hour for me! (*Weeps*)."

Alternating with this moody discontent is a strain of bitterness, now wryly amusing, again almost Swiftian in its malevolence. All of the pleasures for which she married the Squire have been denied Mrs. Sullen. In their stead she is offered only "Ditches . . . Stiles . . . drinking Fat Ale . . . smoaking Tobacco . . ." and soliciting the butler as dancing partner if he will condescend. After a day of oppressive boredom, Mrs. Sullen notes that ". . . my whole Night's Comfort is the tuneable Serenade of the wakeful Nightingale, his Nose. — O the Pleasure of counting the melancholy Clock by a snoring Husband!" But her bitterness is sharper, for instance, when she retorts upon her husband's invitation to acquire a lover provided she does not make him a cuckold: ". . . you would allow me the Sin but rob me of the Pleasure." Her advice to the needy, forlorn woman whose husband has an ailing leg and who is applying to Lady Bountiful for aid and advice has a sadistic twist: ". . . lay your Husbands Leg upon a Table, and with a Choping-knife, you must lay it open as broad as you can; then you must take out the Bone, and beat the Flesh soundly with a rowling-pin . . . season it very well; then rowl it up like Brawn, and put it into the Oven for two Hours."

It is this alternation of melancholy with gaiety, humor with bitterness, and pathos with wit that makes Mrs. Sullen too complicated a human being for laughter only. In still another way, she is a departure from the traditional Restoration female with an unsatisfying husband. Whereas in the plays of Wycherley and Congreve the dissatisfied wife had no hesitation in making a cuckold of her husband, Mrs. Sullen, a voluptuous but hesitating beauty, balances inclination and scruple. For all of her insinuating confidences and erotic innuendo, she remains the conventional wife in behavior, passionately yearning but prudently unyielding. In this conflict, she marks a break with the character of traditional comedy, in which adultery was simply another convention alternative with fidelity to the marriage vow. Mrs. Sullen's attitude is not so coolly simple and straightforward.

The difference makes her vulnerable to criticism as a satisfactory character. Instead of the tartly witty sex-comedy of cuckoldom, we now have a "busom-heaving," tormented, sighing spirit, tempered with inconvenient but obstinate scruples. Gone is the easy, unhesitating, light love of the old Utopia of Restoration gallantry. Mrs. Sullen's attitude is passionate and lusciously languishing. She begins thinking Archer "a very pretty Fellow," next decides, "I like him," then proceeds to wish him "in a Design upon my self." To Archer's light-hearted flattery and artificial rhetoric, she responds not with witty repartee but with a longing sigh: "Had it been my Lot to have match'd with such a Man!" She then drifts to the languishing stage: "I do love that Fellow; — and if I met him . . . undrest . . . Look 'ye Sister . . . I can't swear I cou'd resist the Temptation . . ." Unable to dismiss this particular form of erotic yearning, Mrs. Sullen approaches the frontiers of swoondom when she is questioned by Dorinda. The latter casually asks her whether, if Archer were in her bedchamber, she might not capitulate. On a flood-tide of longing which submerges wit and imagination, Mrs. Sullen returns to her obsession: "Here! what, in my Bed-chamber at two a Clock o' th' Morning, I undress'd, the Family asleep, my hated Husband abroad, and my lovely Fellow at my Feet — O gad, Sister!" This O-gad-Sister attitude inclines towards the sentimental, romantic adultery of enchantment, not the

Restoration adultery of comic detachment.

As such, it might look better in the sober costume of serious domestic drama, unadorned with the cap and bells of jesting comedy. Notwithstanding, it is just this snarled, complicated gathering of human emotions that makes Mrs. Sullen, if not the ideal character of comedy, an ideal role for the actress. The part remains to this day the favorite of actresses and perhaps the principal role of the play.

CONCLUSION: THE PLAY AS "PROBLEM" PLAY

Although not listed under the *Dramatis Personae*, the shadowy presence of John Milton inhabits the world of *The Beaux' Stratagem*. Milton is the ghost-writer of parts of the more impressive dialogue denouncing the indissoluble marriage contract that binds antagonistic personalities in spiritual squalor. Farquhar has pieced out his dialogue with odds and ends stolen out of Milton's holy writ *The Doctrine and Discipline of Divorce*. The cathedral cadences of Milton's voice invade momentarily even the dense breast of Squire Sullen. He merely quotes Milton when he says of the plight of the incompatible couple, "One Flesh! rather two Carcasses join'd unnaturally together." In the same idiom Sir Charles Freeman preaches to Boniface on the difference between the union of mere "Guts" and that union of "rational Creatures" who "have minds."

When Mrs. Sullen sonorously declaims against an irrevocable marriage-bond, she at times almost quotes Milton's attack upon the social will to shackle the supple, shifting life of instinct by the rigid artifice of human law: "Law! what Law can search into the remote Abyss of Nature? what Evidence can prove the unaccountable Disaffections of Wedlock? — Can a Jury sum up the endless Aversions that are rooted in our Souls . . . ?"

When Dorinda (to provide an opening for one of Milton's main preoccupations) suggests that the law "meddles" only in cases of adultery or "uncleanness," Mrs. Sullen again echoes Milton; "Uncleanness! O Sister, casual Violation is a transient Injury, and may possibly be repair'd, but can radical Hatreds, be ever reconcil'd? — No, no, Sister, Nature is the first Lawgiver, and when she has set Tempers opposite, not all the golden Links of Wedlock, nor iron Manacles of Law can keep 'um fast." Notwithstanding, in the course of the play, Mrs. Sullen (helped by Dorinda) is much busier avoiding "casual Violation" even though only a "transient Injury" than in meditating upon the marriage of true minds. It was Farquhar who had read and admired Milton, not Mrs. Sullen — who would have sympathized with Milton's wife.

The casual reader could and the careful one would note that this lofty judicial voice must have been tuned to an instrument other than the mind and spirit of the pleasure-seeking Mrs. Sullen. Her own normal style of allusion to her husband and matrimonial problems is expressed as follows: "O Sister, Sister! I shall never ha' the Good of the Beast till I get him to Town; London, dear London, is the Place for managing and breaking a Husband . . . No, no, Child 'tis a standing Maxim in conjugal Discipline, that . . . when a Lady would be arbitrary with her Husband, she wheedles her Booby up to Town . . . O Dorinda, Dorinda! a fine Woman may do anything in London." It is locality that disturbs Mrs. Sullen, not law.

Quite obviously Mrs. Sullen does not approach her own problem in the spirit of a Mrs. Alving — by reading "advanced" literature. Her private doctrine of conjugal discipline for dealing with "Booby" and "Beast" is not that of Milton's *Discipline*. Her voice is that of the disgruntled stage-wife in a disaffected mood, the conventional voice of the theatre of her time. Her oc-

casionally borrowed voice, that of Milton, is the revolu-
tionary voice of the radical and turbulent seventeenth
century. All the harmonizing skill of Farquhar barely
reconciles the austere elevation of the Miltonic inflec-
tion with the racy vernacular idiom of the thwarted
lady of pleasure and fashion.

We have already dwelt on the bleak situation of the
dying Farquhar as he bent close to his life's brief candle
for light enough for one more play. In such a plight, it
is not surprising that he needed literary help as well as
financial. Wilks supplied the latter; Milton the former.
Yet Farquhar also vividly retouched important elements of plot and situation borrowed from his successful predecessor Sir John Vanbrugh. Farquhar's mind
naturally reverted in his last extremity to his days of
high hope when he first arrived in London, when the
plays in vogue were Vanbrugh's *The Relapse* and *The
Provok'd Wife*.

Whereas in *The Relapse* the bedroom sex-comedy
scene ends in successful seduction, Farquhar using the
same situation forbids. Midnight burglars enter as the
fortuitous custodians of virtue. From *The Provok'd
Wife* Farquhar appears to have borrowed important
elements of plot and character. Besides the basic resemblance of the main characters in both plays, Farquhar's
Dorinda and Aimwell are a revision and re-issue of
Vanbrugh's romantic and non-married couple Bellinda
and Heartfree — only they are no longer treated in the
tradition variously known as the Gay Couple or the
Love Game. Farquhar introduces the newer note of
sentimental reformation of heart and makes the relation more solemn and serious. Last night's wild oats are
sown. But the harvest yields wholesome and nutritious
porridge for next morning's breakfast. Farquhar takes
his couple to the altar not in lightness of heart but in
a mood of lofty sobriety. Rather obviously Vanbrugh's
Sir John and Lady Brute are an early version of the

married couple living in the same state of reciprocal
torment in which we find Squire and Mrs. Sullen, except that London is exchanged for the country. Dorinda, too, is the agreeable confidante to Mrs. Sullen as
is Bellinda to Lady Brute. But Dorinda is more the
moral counsellor, warning against sexual transgression.

In handling the relation between the Squire and
Mrs. Sullen, however, Farquhar had to take into con-
sideration not only the necessary variation upon Vanbrugh to escape the suspicion of servile imitation. He
had also to refrain from contaminating unduly the
newly purified atmosphere of the theatre, the new
climate of feeling brought in by the provoked parson
Collier.

As to the first point, Farquhar has consciously varied
significant details. Indeed he almost appears to have
used a method of negative variation for secondary mat-
ters. For example, Vanbrugh's Lady Brute solemnly dis-
avows any recourse to the expedient of artful coquettry
as an amorous potion to arouse the sluggish emotions
of a negligent husband. Not so Mrs. Sullen. She ar-
ranges the most elaborate plot for just such a purpose.
Or again, when Sir John Brute quite by accident dis-
covers the attentions of another to his wife, he is unwilling to accept the challenge of a duel. Squire Sullen,
deliberately tricked into the triangle situation, is all
for the arbitrament of the sword, despite the fact that
he cherishes only his honor of husband-proprietor,
openly disdaining any interest in either his wife's virtue
or person.

Secondly, Vanbrugh leaves it passingly clear that
Constant who pursues the married Lady Brute (he is
the prototype of Archer) will succeed, that Lady Brute's
husband will be cuckolded not long after the final curtain. Such solutions by 1707 are less tolerable. Indeed,
so astonishingly has the climate of feeling changed that
Anne Oldfield, the actress "discovered" by Farquhar in

a local tavern, objects even to the presumably purified arrangement whereby Mrs. Sullen achieves her freedom. Anne Oldfield objected to the makeshift device whereby Mrs. Sullen was returned again to green pastures. Obviously she did not believe in the "divorce" and felt that it was merely a blind for a possible future adulterous relationship, that it was a clumsy makeshift concocted by Farquhar for a happy curtain.

We have already seen that Farquhar is careful not to allow Archer to seduce Mrs. Sullen in the bedroom scene. Besides the new climate of morality, Farquhar has to reckon with an element of plot — Mrs. Sullen's rural isolation. If Archer is not to prevail against her virtue, neither can she be left alone in the sole company of the Squire, her husband. Farquhar's sense of comedy required a happy ending. Vanbrugh's Lady Brute was in London. As Mrs. Sullen enviously reflected, in London a wife "may do anything." But not in the provinces. Archer even as an interim lover would soon be on his way. A genuine opportunist and adventurer, Archer would not tarry long in Lichfield, especially now that he had acquired a small fortune with which to invest in the pleasures of London. What then was Farquhar to do as an alternative to returning his favorite character to the abhorrent and abhorring husband?

What he did was to borrow from Paul to pay the interest due on the sum previously borrowed from Peter. From Milton could be borrowed what was needed to vary the borrowing from Vanbrugh. Milton's *Doctrine and Discipline* would supply the ready-made phrases and a device of plot whereby the Restoration comedy of *The Provok'd Wife* could be transformed into the nearly sentimental comedy of the unyoked wife. The device was to introduce divorce or separation by "mutual consent."

That the Miltonic borrowings are an expedient for a

happy curtain (and not a new social epoch) is evident in the supreme hurry and carelessness with which Farquhar introduces the question, quite without any of the early and careful preparation of an Ibsen. Sir Charles Freeman is the *deus ex machina* who, at the last minute, descends upon the play from the empty spaces over the stage. He arrives as a plausible means for awarding Mrs. Sullen her "divorce" and her liberty. He too has gotten up his Milton and talks about the union of true minds although neither Mrs. Sullen nor the Squire has the slightest interest in the sort of mental union celebrated and desired by Milton. Equally unprepared for is the introduction at the last moment of something called Squire Sullen's "writings" which can presumably be used to coerce his consent although there has been talk about "mutual consent."

Sir Charles Freeman, a brother of Mrs. Sullen, is neither a member of Parliament, a representative of the Church, nor a part of the judicial system. That is, he belongs to no portion of the governing order which would be responsible for evaluating and passing judgment on the proposals he is to make. He has been simply waiting off-stage, Milton in hand, for his cue. Even Archer, who stands to gain most from the transaction refuses to regard "mutual consent" seriously. He treats it as an uproarious joke. Despite his drafting of Miltonic phrases and attitudes for service in *The Beaux' Stratagem*, Farquhar is very unlikely to have had in mind the role of a proto-Ibsen. Almost certainly he was not using the stage as a platform for sensational social reform, heroically expounding the evils of a too rigid matrimonial law. Milton might be regarded as a forerunner of Ibsen, not Farquhar. To vary a notable metaphor in its application, what Farquhar admired in Milton's divorce pamphlet was the gorgeous plumage, not the dying bird. He merely wanted a few colorful feathers for the nest of a happy ending.

In *Lady Windermere's Fan*, Oscar Wilde presumably borrows from Cardinal Newman's "Autobiographical Memoir" the materials for philosophizing on the "evangelical conscience." He uses these materials to give flavor to his play and point to his plot, not because he has embraced the moral philosophy of the High Church movement. Farquhar was not more seriously interested in adopting and establishing Milton's philosophy of divorce than was Wilde in renovating England with Newman's theory of conscience. Milton's volcanic outpouring, fired by a personal and domestic tragedy, could be used to ornament and conclude a social comedy. With his gift for felicitous handling of improbable materials, Farquhar did just that.

Much, if not most, of the standard criticism of Farquhar's comedy is contrary to the foregoing. Milton's presence in the play, however tenuous, has given it a thematic character in the eyes of many contemporary critics of note. Not to notice such a tradition of interpretation would be a culpable negligence in any serious account of the play and its place in the tradition of English comedy.

The comedy of misreading (as we think) Farquhar's comedy began with the Victorian A. W. Ward. His massive reflections in three volumes (*History of English Drama to the Death of Queen Anne*) came to a second edition in 1899. In the course of his treatment of Farquhar, Ward condemned him in general as a man of "coarse" fibre and "offensive" lapses of taste. A critic of note, William Archer, came to Farquhar's defense. Although he stands at the gateway of modern criticism in a limited respect, Archer is mainly late Victorian in his preoccupations. In rescuing Farquhar from Ward's moral accusations, Archer reminds one at moments of another late Victorian, the eminent Gilbert Murray, editor and translator of Greek dramatists for his generation. Murray, casting about a little desperately, succeeded in elevating his favored Athenians above the Romans by observing that the former were "more indecent but less lascivious" than the latter. Within slightly less equivocal limits and with a greatly expanded rhetoric, Archer established a violent moral contrast between Farquhar and earlier Restoration dramatists.

In Archer's criticism there was much of the rattle and clatter of the Victorian moralist. He appears to be trying to do for the stage what Carlyle had attempted for the age — detonate a resounding affirmation of moral values in the shrinking world of late-Victorian religious belief. Archer — and others to follow him — begin to treat Farquhar much as an unctuous modern revivalist might a particularly colorful convert, one snatched from a morally distressed, sin-saturated area, a convert whose limited purity shone in contrast to the lurid vice of his companions and surroundings: Prince Hal's "bright metal on a sullen ground." In general, Archer gives us a character of Farquhar not unlike that of Farquhar's Aimwell of the present play: a bit of a rake, but a man whose heart is good and whose head is sound.

On the more specific issue of *The Beaux' Stratagem*, Ward expressed in a tone suitable to a family-minded generation his horror at Farquhar's frivolous and irresponsible treatment of the sanctity of the marriage contract. But *The Beaux' Stratagem* was the very play in which Archer felt that Farquhar had come clean and decent. What Ward specifically denounced, Archer delighted in. In order to delight in it, Archer had first to moralize it. But the form of his moralizing took a particular late-Victorian coloring. What is of significance for so much of the criticism of *The Beaux' Stratagem* ever since is the fact that the shadow of Ibsen falls sharply across the path by which Archer — admirer and editor of Ibsen — has returned to Farquhar's play.

In his determination to detach Farquhar morally

from the Restoration dramatists, Archer laments his early death, noting "the steady growth we can perceive in him, not only of moral feeling, but of sober criticism of life." Having thus brought Farquhar closer to the age of Arnold, Archer comes to Ward's specific grievance, Farquhar's frivolous treatment of divorce and separation. Archer defends this element of the plot not as a specimen of irresponsible gaiety but, to the contrary, as "a remarkable proof of the increasing earnestness of his outlook upon life . . . a serious and very damaging criticism of the conventional view that there can be no immorality in marriage save breach of the marriage vow. These scenes are, in fact, a plea for what Farquhar regarded, rightly or wrongly, as a more rational law of divorce." Archer continues: "When Farquhar seriously (and wittily) set himself to show that a certain type of marriage was loathsome and immoral, he broke once for all with the irresponsible licentiousness of his school. He admitted a moral standard, and subjected social convention, not to mere cynical persiflage, but to the criticism of reason." Archer, having armed Farquhar with the banner of reform, then bade him charge the barricades.

The wave of Ibsenite interpretation set in motion by such a declaration has rolled with mounting crescendo to the shores of the present. The attitude has since been tacitly accepted or explicitly endorsed by scholars, historians, critics, and glowingly expanded by biographers. Among the critics and scholars who give the interpretation support or at least tolerance are Mr. Frederic S. Boas and Mr. Bonamy Dobrée. Among the social historians are Dr. Alleman. The scholars are represented by Dr. Larson, who first directed attention to Farquhar's quite liberal borrowings from Milton's *Doctrine and Discipline*. Then with an ardent cheerfulness exceeding even Archer's, Mr. Willard Connely, Farquhar's recent and most fluent biographer, elaborates upon Archer's thesis with a perorative warmth.

In his recent lively biography, Mr. Connely caps the tradition in such unhesitating words as "It now seemed proper to Farquhar and necessary for the good of the public, to reach boldly beyond all precedent in Restoration comedy, and to bring the concrete discussion of divorce upon the stage." With the same independence of supporting reference or analysis, Mr. Connely has added to Farquhar's private moral growth the note of *pro bono publico.* Then Mr. Connely, continuing to exercise the freedom of the biographical novelist, takes us even closer: "Then Farquhar got down to the question that was really on his mind: what to do with a man and wife who were mutually and hopelessly antipathetic . . ." Now in fact Farquhar, in the hours remaining to him before his own divorce from life, was in considerable anguish to make some provision in pounds and shillings for the indigent wife and children who would survive him. Ignoring this oppressive fact, Farquhar's biographer assures us that the dying man "flouted like Milton the inanity of convention, re-stated Milton's case for reform in the law of divorce, and invited his own forthcoming audience to accept the solution by which the play was to end."

Obviously such a view implies clearly, if not startlingly, that Farquhar was the inventor of the social conscience and the thesis play, that *The Beaux' Stratagem* embodies a brilliant and conscious innovation: the use of the theatre as a vehicle of specific social criticism and domestic reform. In one way or another the views of many varying critics point to Farquhar as a prototype of Ibsen: depending upon the individual enthusiasm, something in between the cautious, moralizing Ibsen of Professor Joseph Wood Krutch and the fervent, crusading Ibsen of Bernard Shaw. At any rate, Farquhar's treatment of the wrangling and abusive relation of the Sullens is to such critics not so much a highly qualified variation of the comedy of Vanbrugh as an unqualified anticipation of the comedy of Ibsen. The Quintessence of *The Beaux' Stratagem* is a bold assault upon the unduly rigid and stifling regulations governing marriage.

Despite the impressive names ranged upon the other side of the question, it seems to us that Farquhar no more sought to use his play to liberalize the laws governing divorce than he sought to insinuate socialism with the phrases concerning poverty which Shaw found convenient to borrow from him. For all of that, *Ghosts* are now confidently reported as wandering about the midnight terrain of early eighteenth-century Lichfield.

Actually, both internal and external evidence is contrary to such a conception. First there is the fact of contemporary silence concerning any such introduction, "boldly" or otherwise, of so serious a proposition into drama. We all know of the angry buzz and flutter of excitement that greeted Ibsen's handling of the theme in *The Doll's House* and *Ghosts,* of the angry agitation surrounding Milton's bulky tract. Indeed, we have seen that not even Anne Oldfield could quite take it seriously. Clearly she considered the "mutual consent" merely a sophistical device for escaping Squire Sullen. Apparently Farquhar did himself, for he is reported to have consoled her by promising to give her a "real" divorce. One cannot imagine Milton or Ibsen lightheartedly setting aside their passionate polemics as a joking matter.

The critics who regard the drama as presenting the divorce-by-mutual-consent thesis attempt to make much of Farquhar's marriage. They insist that he married in hope of capturing an heiress, that the lady deceived him, and that his consequent disappointment prompted in part his plea for more liberal divorce laws. Certainly there was passionate personal prompting behind Milton's tract. But all of the tradition of the time that has reached us is to the effect that Farquhar and his wife handsomely suited each other and lived in mutual sympathy.

Internally the evidence is even more dubious. The idea of divorce is most casually introduced at the last moment and has on the face of it the appearance of a mere improvisation of plot, not an improvement of the human lot. Nor do the characters in any way illustrate the kind of situation which Milton had in mind when writing the tract from which Farquhar borrowed phrases. What Milton was contemplating was the union of a Samuel Taylor Coleridge with a Sara Fricker — the tormented romantic genius tethered irrevocably to a plump suburban matron permanently in front of a television set. The only issue between Squire and Mrs. Sullen is drink, tavern, and horses as opposed to teas, gossip, and cards. This is not Milton's dramatic struggle in which "spirit" is hobbled and fettered by union with gross "matter." Mrs. Sullen is neither a Nora Helmer nor a Mrs. Alving.

But to conclude the matter. If one wished to discover Farquhar's purpose — or that of any other eighteenth-century dramatist — where would he apply but to the Prologue and Epilogue of the play? And there one is confronted with a desolating silence. As likewise by the "Advertisement." The discovery of Archer and the elaborations of subsequent critics seem not to have touched the mind of author or audience. If Farquhar, so conscious of addressing himself to so momentous a question, was really so engaged, why is there complete silence about this intention in the Prologue? Why, to the contrary, does the Prologue contain lines such as the following:

When thro' Great Britain's fair extensive Round,
The Trumps of Fame the Notes of Union sound;
When Anna's Scepter points the Laws their Course,

And Her Example gives her Precepts Force:
There scarce is room for Satyr, all our Lays
Must be, or Songs of Triumph, or of Praise.

Surely so witty a man as Farquhar would have sensed the ironic equivocation of Trumps of Fame sounding "Notes of Union" when writing a stage plea for divorce. Never did Prologue so totally abdicate its function if this murmur of general complacency was intended to be a trumpet call to matrimonial reform. Epilogue and Advertisement stress but one point: Farquhar hoped that his play would be successful entertainment.

Dr. Johnson said that much could be done with a Scotsman if he were caught early enough. England has done well with her Irishmen of talent and wit from Farquhar to Wilde. But not even Queen Anne's England could Miltonize George Farquhar. The critics are interpreting Farquhar as one might have interpreted a well-known remark of Dr. Johnson's if it had been found as a pencilled note in the fly-leaf of his copy of Milton's *Doctrine and Discipline*:

It is so far from being natural for a man and woman to live in a state of marriage that we find all the motives which they have for remaining in that condition and the restraints which civilized society imposes to prevent separation, are hardly sufficient to keep them together.

In such a supposed context the passage might be regarded as an expression of dignified sarcasm in behalf of Milton's views. Rather it merely reflects Johnson's sturdy, unsentimental realism of mind, his frank view of a system which he accepted with an almost fatal resignation.

Farquhar too knew that he lived in an age in which it was rare for even a powerful nobleman to pass his private Parliamentary bill for a divorce. The notion of making such an exclusive prerogative as accessible as the country air of Lichfield was hardly thinkable. But where Dr. Johnson was realistic, Farquhar was whimsical. To grace a final curtain with a pleasing vista, Farquhar would create over the ruined site of the Restoration's Utopia of gallantry the transitory vision of a Utopia of easy divorce.

The Staging

The first performance of Farquhar's *The Beaux' Strata-gem* took place in the Queen's Theatre, Haymarket, on March 8, 1707. This was in a period of agitation for dramatic reform, and the very existence of the Queen's Theatre, as well as of Farquhar's play, is an interesting index of the changes that were taking place. The building had been designed in 1705 by the famous architect and playwright, Sir John Vanbrugh, creator of Blenheim Palace and *The Relapse*. Vanbrugh's architecture, like his plays, was witty and stylized in the spirit of the Stuart courtiers who had been his chief patrons. But now, perhaps encouraged by the radically Protestant reign of William and Mary (1689-1702), Puritanical voices were chastising this spirit with new vigor and effect. Extremists no doubt felt that Blenheim was too ostentatious to be completely virtuous; but Blenheim was to shelter a national hero, the Duke of Marlborough, and was seldom accused of outright vice. On the other hand, plays like *The Relapse* were hardly heroic, and their bold-spoken wit provoked frequent charges of obscenity. The most important attack, *A Short View of the Immorality and Profaneness of the English Stage*, was written by Jeremy Collier in 1698. In this *The Relapse* was honored with a section to itself.

Many critics were calling for the abolition of theatres entirely. But Queen Anne, with a happy diffidence, seems to have been interested neither in abolishing nor in attending plays. She was persuaded to try and reform them, however, and for this purpose she licensed "a

New Company of Comedians" whose home was to be in Vanbrugh's new building. The Queen was not a merry monarch, but she was a Stuart, and possibly she may have relished a little the irony of assigning the patent to Vanbrugh and to William Congreve, who was almost equally ill-thought-of in Puritan circles. In any case, the new license charged two of the villains of Collier's *Short View* with responsibility for theatrical reform. Collier's heirs, the Society for the Reformation of Manners, did not think it was funny. " 'Tis impossible," they cried, "that Her Majesty should act so directly contrary to the End she proposed, as to commit the Management of a State to that very Man [Vanbrugh], who Debauch'd it to a degree beyond the Looseness of all former Times . . ."

Despite the Queen's curious choice of watchdogs, reform did occur. Or at least the comedies of the new century were to be less lusty than those of the old. But another and more significant result of the establishment of the new company was not new purity but new commercialism. The theatre of the Restoration had been in large part financed by the Court. But recently, under William and Mary and then under Anne, Court support had ended. Theatrical managers now had to depend almost exclusively on the public sale of seats. Moreover, Vanbrugh's building became London's third large theatre and so increased competition that managers were forced to seek out new audiences in new places, and, as *The Beaux' Stratagem* will show, to woo these audiences with something new in the way of entertainment. And so it was that Vanbrugh and Congreve discovered that they were no longer courtiers amusing a small group of aristocrats, but unwilling businessmen engaged in a risky trade.

At the beginning, they were unaware of this. Their first intention was to produce Italian opera, and their theatre therefore sought to rival the sumptuous houses of the Continent. It was like nothing ever seen in England before, very different from the modest playhouses in Drury Lane and Lincoln's Inn Fields. To the street it presented a small, sedate façade divided into a triple arcade on the ground floor. This was surmounted by a matching rank of windows suggesting the *piano nobile* of an Italian palace, and above this was a third floor consisting of three oval oculi. The whole front was treated with heavy cornices and string-courses, and was formed of solid, respectable London brick enhanced by massive stone quoins. It could have been the façade of a church or a public hall. This aroused the disgust of Puritan-minded critics like Defoe, who objected to what they saw as architectural hypocrisy:

> View but our Stately Pile, the Columns stand
> Like some Great Council Chamber of the Land:
> When Strangers View the Beauty and the State,
> As they pass by, they ask "What Church is that?"
> Thinking a Nation, so Devout as we,
> Ne'er built such Domes, but to some Deity.

But alas, sighs the poet, what gods are worshipped inside? To these critics the grandeur of the interior must have been even more painful than the misleading primness of the outside. Unfortunately, we have no specific information, no drawings or engravings, to show us exactly what this interior was like. Laurence Whistler, who has provided the documents on which this account is based, has assembled what information there is in his interesting book on Vanbrugh (see Bibliography). Colossal pilasters rose around the walls of the auditorium and supported a rich entablature which joined the crest of an elliptical proscenium arch on the stage wall. Midway between floor and ceiling were tiers of boxes arranged in sweeping horse-shoe curves, and overhead was a dome.

To theatre professionals all this magnificence was not

so much immoral as impractical. The most famous actor and manager of the time, Colly Cibber, later complained:

> Almost every proper quality and convenience of a good theatre had been sacrificed, or neglected, to shew the spectator a vast triumphal piece of architecture! For what could their vast columns, their gilded cornices, their immoderate high roofs avail, when scarce one word in ten could be distinctly heard in it? This extraordinary and superfluous space occasion'd such an undulation, from the voice of every actor, that generally what they said sounded like the gabbling of so many people in the lofty aisles of a cathedral.

Thus to the offense of Puritans and professionals respectively Vanbrugh sacrificed propriety and acoustics for sheer unadulterated grandeur. But far from disdaining this new means of attracting patrons, later managers have followed Vanbrugh's lead and vied with each other in the creation of "extraordinary and superfluous spaces" whose purpose has been to overwhelm as well as to entertain the audience.

There is another point of interest in the Queen's Theatre. We should note its novel location in the Haymarket, which at the time was full of the houses of hatters and wine-merchants, though it was also near St. James's Palace. Not only did the establishment of the new company mark the beginning of an increase in the number of theatres and thereby intensify competition. It also marked the beginning of a move from aristocratic to middle-class precincts. Perhaps Vanbrugh located his building near the Palace in the hope of whetting the Queen's interest in drama. But when this did not happen, later managers turned to the lesser but more numerous fry who also lived in the neighborhood. This maneuver was successful, and within a short time the Haymarket saw another theatre, the so-called Little French House. Soon there were still more new theatres in Lincoln's Inn Fields, in Covent Garden, and in Goodman's Fields, all in active competition. Nor was it long before provincial towns began to build theatres. These usually appeared at first in fashionable resorts like Bath, Norwich, and Tunbridge Wells. In time the idea passed to the colonies, and as early as 1716 Williamsburg had a theatre, and there were others later on in Charleston, Philadelphia, and New York. All of these buildings may be thought of as marks of the new commercial spirit in the English theatre, a spirit that had been born with the death of the Court-oriented Restoration drama.

Since provincial and colonial audiences, like those now in London, were mainly composed of middle-class people, productions were soon being tailored to their taste. The early history of the Queen's Theatre is a case in point. One realization that was forced almost immediately on Vanbrugh and Congreve was that Haymarket audiences did not want Italian opera. The first production, *The Loves of Ergasto,* ran only five nights. And so the managers turned to plays. Two of these, both produced in 1705, were by Vanbrugh himself: *The Confederacy* and *The Mistake,* the latter being a translation of Molière's *Le Dépit Amoureux.* Both were typical Restoration comedies, full of double-entendres and rapid-fire verbal wit. They were no doubt somewhat beyond the ken of the tired businessmen who came to see them and were no more popular than *The Loves of Ergasto.* Indeed, it was not until *The Beaux' Stratagem* itself was produced in 1707 that the Queen's Theatre stopped losing money. Possibly it is significant that just before this the courtly Vanbrugh had leased his share of the patent, and the theatre was temporarily in the hands of a company from Drury Lane backed by Christopher Rich. Rich's approach to the theatre was notably non-aristocratic, and *The Beaux' Stratagem* was successful. It had many performances at the Queen's and elsewhere, and by 1808 had been revived no less than nineteen times. Apparently, it was the sort of play the new audiences in Vanbrugh's new theatre wanted. What does *The Beaux Stratagem* have that the *The Mistake* does not have?

The first thing we notice is a change in the nature of the comic materials. Farquhar's play has plenty of comedy, but much of it is implied rather than stated, and much of it consists of the actor's visual and spontaneous humor rather than the self-conscious verbal wit of the author which was the standard fare of Restoration comedy. In fact, like many subsequent English plays, *The Beaux' Stratagem* was conceived as a vehicle for specific performers who brought to their roles all kinds of favorite mannerisms, gestures, and comic turns. The part of Archer was written for the most famous comedian of the period, Robert Wilks, and Dorinda was written for his feminine counterpart Mrs. Anne Oldfield. When Farquhar did this, he was only repeating what he had done before in *A Trip to the Jubilee* (Drury Lane, 1699) where Wilks was an immense success as the memorable Sir Harry Wildair. Steele's criticism of this play gives us a good idea of the kind of "actor's theatre" that was coming into existence. "The Dialogue," he wrote, "in it self has something too low to bear a Criticism upon it: but Mr. *Wilks* enters into the Part with so much Skill, that the Gallantry, the Youth, and Gaiety of a young Man of plentiful Fortune, is looked upon with as much Indulgence on the Stage, as in real Life, without any of those Intermixtures of Wit and Humour, which usually prepossess us in Favour of such Characters in other Plays." Apparently, Farquhar did not consider this a nasty remark, as earlier writers might have done. At least he himself says much the same sort of thing in the "Advertisement" to *The Beaux' Stratagem*. Here he attributes the success of the piece, and the removal of its faults, to the "Amends made in the Representation" by Wilks.

An example of the kind of visual "amends" that Wilks very probably made is found in Archer's first scene, where he and Aimwell appear at the inn to discuss their escapade. In this scene Farquhar supplies Archer with what amounts to a series of impersonations. There are Jack Handicraft, the "handsome, well-dress'd, mannerly, sharping Rogue," Nick Marabone, riding in the coach he formerly sat behind as footman, Jack Generous in his "Autumnal Periwig, shading his melancholy Face," and so on. The realization of this sort of comedy lay in Wilks' mimicry, his "business," and his general cavorting around stage as he manufactured a spontaneous comic scene using the script as a scenario. Such clowning and ad-libing were extremely common, and indeed whole speeches were sometimes interpolated even into serious plays, as Allardyce Nicholl tells us in his *History of the Eighteenth Century Drama*. "You are never to perplex the drama with speeches extempore," says Mrs. Clinket in Gay, Pope, and Arbuthnot's *Three Hours after Marriage* (Drury Lane, 1717). "Madam," is the reply, " 'tis what the top players often do."

Aside from the fact that it had a wider appeal than verbal wit, the new tendency to visual comedy and improvisation was strengthened by the popularity of the Italian *commedia dell'arte*. These improvised dramas, using standard characters like Harlequin and Columbine, consisted very largely of what today would be called "sight gags." And then English performers were turning more and more to that still popular and entirely speechless form, the pantomime. An early form of vaudeville was also in vogue. On June 8, 1703, for example, Rich's Drury Lane Company presented a play by Cibber with the following additional attraction: "The famous Mr. *Clynch* of *Barnet*" who was to give "an imitation of the *Organ* with 3 Voices, the Double Curtel [a kind of bassoon], and the *Bells*, the *Huntsman* with his *Horn* and *Pack* of *Dogs;* All which he performs with his Mouth on the open Stage." Managers frequently added this sort of thing to their productions of legitimate plays in the form of interludes and afterpieces. But it is not hard to imagine how soon these relatively low-brow amusements began to affect the acting of the plays themselves.

It is in this atmosphere of reformed manners, novel architectural grandeur, a new sort of middle-class entertainment, that we must try to imagine the early performances of *The Beaux' Stratagem*. Let us now see if we can reconstruct a few of the more specific circumstances that attended them.

First of all, the audience entered the theatre on a first-come, first-served basis, there being no tickets or reserved seats. You purchased a brass token which was given to one of the "gatherers" stationed at each entrance to the auditorium. A rich man could send his footman to buy box seats and hold them until his master arrived, but if you decided for the orchestra, or pit as it was called, it was simply a scramble for the seats nearest the front. There was a great deal more comfort in a box, for these were furnished with movable chairs, and were actually small parlors where you chatted, drank tea, and greeted other box-holders. If you wanted to have a private conversation, there were curtains which could be drawn across the front of the box to keep out the distracting spectacle on stage. The modern notion that an audience should sit perfectly still was unheard of.

But this does not mean that the audience paid no attention to the play. We have already seen how popular certain actors were, and we can be sure that during important scenes they were heard out. In fact, the audience's judgment of a play's worth, especially on the first night, was final. If a play was disliked, the manager was informed of this by a chorus of boos and hisses when he stepped out in front of the curtain at the end of the piece. He would thereupon announce that the play was not to be performed again — or he would simply retire in the face of pandemonium. If he received applause, though, he would announce that the play was to be repeated until further notice. This explains why prologues and epilogues begged so frankly for applause. In the epilogue to *The Beaux' Stratagem*, Farquhar goes so far as to urge his mortal illness:

If to our Play your Judgment can't be kind,
Let its expiring Author Pity find.

It was especially important to authors that their plays receive at least three performances, for the third was traditionally the "author's benefit" and it was not until then that he received any substantial payment. Not only did authors ask, often rather poignantly, for applause; they often took more certain measures by hiring claques. Actors did the same thing. The presence of these claques produced tense and sometimes riotous results. Both actors and authors were frequently in the pay of political parties, and so if a Whig author hired a claque to applaud his play, patriotic Tories would form an anti-claque to hiss it off the stage. This tendentious atmosphere was added to by the presence of gangs of young men who merely wanted to make bi-partisan noise. Nicholl tells us that one poor author, the Rev. James Miller, was so unfortunate as to offend a contingent of law clerks from the Temple with certain lines in his farce *An Hospital for Fools* (Drury Lane, 1739). Nicholl quotes an account of the first and only performance, where "one single Word was not heard that the Actors spoke, the Noise of these First-Night Gentlemen was so great; however the Actors went thro' it, and the Spectators might see their Mouths wag, and that was all." Such tumults, added to the "undulations" in the actors' voices due to bad acoustics, strengthen our assertion that the visual part of the drama counted for a good deal.

The stages of London theatres at this time were much like ours, except that the apron was extremely deep, projecting well out into the auditorium, a relic of the pre-Commonwealth public theatres like Shakespeare's Globe. The apron spread across the entire width of the auditorium and on either side was a pair of doors (sometimes only one and at other times three) leading backstage. Most of the entrances were made through these proscenium doors, though some were made through the wings, and almost all the action took place on the apron. Above the proscenium doors were boxes or balconies which could serve for part of the action or accommodate members of the audience, depending on the requirements of the piece. Across the back of the apron hung the curtain, just behind the proscenium arch. At the beginning of the performance, the curtain would rise and hang in decorative festoons just above the arch. There was no dimming of lights, and the curtain remained up during the entire performance, no attempt being made to mask changes of scene. The scenery itself consisted of light wooden frames called "flats," just as it does today. Not only the walls of the inn in Act I, but most of the furniture and other dressings would be painted directly on the scenery. There were seldom practicable doors and windows as we have them today, and no cycloramas, backing pieces, and so on. The illusion of reality had to be achieved entirely by the quality of the scene-painting. The arrangement of flats was standardized: high, narrow pieces called "wings" were set parallel to the audience on either side of the stage in pairs. Across the back, forming a rear wall, were wider flats called shutters (see diagram). Behind each pair of wings, and behind the rear shutters, were additional pieces with other scenes painted on them. When the scene changed to the large

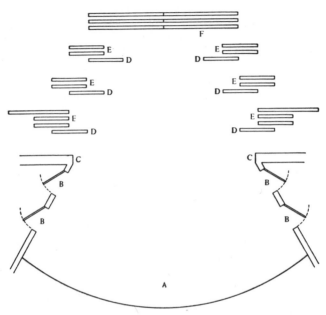

Sketch-Plan of Drury Lane, c. 1700

Drury Lane is illustrated rather than the Queen's Theatre, since we have no accurate plans of the latter. *A* is
the large apron upon which most of the action takes
place. *B* indicates the proscenium doors. *C* is the proscenium opening itself behind which the curtain hangs.
The onstage wings (inn) are indicated by the letter *D*,
and the offstage wings, ready to be pushed on when the
scene changes to the room in Lady Bountiful's house
(ACT III, SCENE 3), are marked *E*. Behind the first set of
wings is a set of shutters which can close completely for
small scenes such as the gallery in Lady Bountiful's
house (Act II, Scene 1). The rear shutters are marked *F*.

room in Lady Bountiful's house (Act III, Scene 3), the onstage wings (D in the plan) would have been pulled offstage and the second set of scenery (E) pushed on. The same would happen to the shutters (F). The third full scene, the bed-chamber, would then follow in due course; and the fourth (Act V, Scene 3), "another apartment in the same house," could conceivably have been on a fourth set, but in such situations the former set of wings would probably remain in place, and only the shutters be changed. The extra shutters behind the downstage (front) set of wings would provide the scenery for the gallery in Lady Bountiful's house (Act II, Scene 1), probably utilizing the same set of downstage wings that would be used for the second full scene.

Frequently, indigent managers kept a single set of wings on stage, painted with some all-purpose decoration such as columns on pedestals, and changed only the back shutters. All flats ran in grooves, the botton grooves being built into the stage floor like railroad tracks and the upper ones hanging on wooden battens. Thus a scene shift was like the movement of a whole group of sliding doors. The stagehands who performed the shift remained out of sight, of course. Across the top of the stage, to mask the upper grooves, wide strips of canvas were hung. These were called "borders" and were usually painted sky blue. They were almost never changed, except in very elaborate productions.

Just as the scenery slid on and off the stage apparently of its own volition, so did the chairs, tables, and other movable properties. Light ropes were attached to the legs of the furniture, and stagehands behind the wings pulled it off. At other times uniformed footmen would walk on stage and change the properties around. But there were few properties in the eighteenth-century theatre, and the actors seldom used them as they do today, sitting down, getting up, walking to a window or mantelpiece, and so on. They seldom got anywhere near the scenery either, most of the dialogue being spoken by the actors standing well out in front on the apron.

The lighting was very simple compared with ours today. Candles are not susceptible of very elaborate effects, and anyway the auditorium chandeliers were kept burning all during the performance, as we have seen. There were usually small candles equipped with reflectors around the downstage edge of the apron — the footlights — and there were also chandeliers between each pair of wings to light the scenery. Occasionally for night scenes these were moved offstage to achieve an effect of dimming light, and colored glass lenses were also used. But in general the scenery and stage proper were rather dim, while the actors on the apron were quite brilliantly lighted.

Costumes were carefully designed to place even more emphasis on the actor. Vanbrugh complains about this in the prologue to *The Mistake*:

> The first Dramatick Rule is, have good Cloaths,
> To charm the gay Spectator's gentle Breast,
> In Lace and Feather Tragedy's express'd,
> And Heroes die unpity'd, if ill-dress'd.

The costumes were always in the current fashion — no one felt it needful to dress Greeks in chitons or Romans in togas. But Orientals, clowns, and tragic heroes did wear distinguishing garb: for example, the latter wore a kind of plumed hat adapted from Roman dress, called a shuttlecock. This is the "Feather" that Vanbrugh is complaining about. There was almost a riot at Drury Lane in the early nineteenth century when John Philip Kemble appeared in Macbeth in a Scottish cap (at the suggestion of Sir Walter Scott) instead of this traditional shuttlecock.

A typical Archer would appear in buckled pumps, probably black; white silk stockings; and tight knee-breeches called *culottes*. He would also wear a long heavy coat reaching to the knees, very full, and decorated with elaborate pockets and enormous deep cuffs in which he kept things like handkerchiefs and snuffboxes. Under the coat he would wear a brocaded waistcoat while a frothy lace stock served as collar and covered his shirtfront, and more lace dangled from his wrists. Unless he was pretty rustic, like Sullen, an early eighteenth-century gentleman wore a very full wig. Men's hats were round-crowned and wide-brimmed, with the brim pinned up on three sides, producing the familiar tricorne. Gentlemen usually carried elegant little swords. Footmen and military officers, such as Aimwell and Count Bellair, would wear ornate uniforms, cut perhaps a little more old-fashionedly than civilian dress, and with gilt frogging across the chest instead of an open coat. Sullen, when he enters at the beginning of Act II, would be in Sunday morning undress: a "Turkish" dressing gown reaching to the floor, and his natural hair hanging loose or concealed by a turban. Foigard, the priest, would not wear distinctive garb, but his civil costume might be black. The lower orders — Gibbet, Hounslow, Boniface, and the rest — would wear simplified homespun versions of their betters' clothes.

Strangely enough, less importance was given to women's costume than to that of the male actors. The actresses wore long skirts stiffened and belled out by hoops that, in 1707, were considerably smaller in diameter than they were to be later on. Bodices were low-waisted and low-necked, very tight and stiffened with bones, and with sleeves that were full and flowing, ending at the elbow in huge bows and dangling lace. Ladies carried fans, which they used to send flirtatious signals, and tiny, elaborate reticules. Like the men they wore elaborate wigs dressed very high. Lady Bountiful, Dorinda, and Mrs. Sullen would wear silk, probably, while

Gipsy and Cherry would wear plainer materials made into simpler dresses with tighter sleeves, the skirts being protected by aprons. Bright colors were not worn by both sexes, but by the gentry only.

It must be admitted that, as a whole, if we could be transported to an early eighteenth-century London and a performance of *The Beaux' Stratagem,* we would miss a good deal of what we get nowadays in the theatre. We would miss the convincing properties and scenic effects which help to establish atmosphere, and the modern lighting which puts the audience in darkness while an entirely separate world takes form on the stage, a world whose brightness and clarity seem almost more than real. We would miss above all the careful co-ordination of movement, speech, and action which to-day's director achieves with his careful rehearsals, and the single unified style with which he is able to inform every detail of the performance. These are all effects which simply did not exist in eighteenth-century pro-ductions, or which the actor had to achieve on his own by means of his body and his voice. A great actor like Wilks, however, used these instruments with a virtuosity and precision that today we associate with the singer or the dancer. In speaking, for example, Wilks must have given enormous attention to pauses, inflections, and changes of tone and rhythm. In an age of great public speaking and great conversation, he would have had an expert and critical audience. We must therefore imagine that as he and Mrs. Oldfield begin to generate the broad comic atmosphere of the play, they will start to rule the turbulent audience. Their familiar and polished repertoires of gestures, grimaces, and speeches will banish animosity and inattention, and a kind of cheerful intimacy will come about, similar to what we often feel today, among the English, when they are watching a favorite music-hall performer.

We have seen that the novel splendor of Vanbrugh's

new building in the Haymarket helped to usher in a new age of middle class entertainment, in which Restoration wit gave place to a more comfortable comedy of clowning and sentiment. With the new emphasis on spontaneous behavior and visual effects, the actor was pre-eminent. We have a similar phenomenon today in that most visual of arts, the movies. And yet Farquhar, in *The Beaux' Stratagem* produced far more than a serviceable scenario, a work whose dialogue has "something too low to bear a Criticism upon it." On the contrary, in reading it today we are still moved by its skill, its gallantry, its youth, its gaiety, and its not infrequent sallies of wit.

ADVERTISEMENT

The reader may find some faults in this play, which my illness prevented the amending of; but there is great amends made in the presentation, which cannot be matched, nor more than the friendly and indefatigable care of Mr. Wilks, to whom I chiefly owe the success of the play.

GEORGE FARQUHAR

Cast of Characters

Synopsis of Scenes

Prologue

spoken by Mr. Wilks[1]

When strife disturbs, or sloth corrupts an age,
Keen satire is the business of the stage.
When the *Plain Dealer*[2] writ, he lashed those crimes
Which then infested most — the modish times:
But now, when faction sleeps and sloth is fled,
And all our youth in active fields are bred;
When through Great Britain's fair extensive round
The trumps of fame the notes of UNION sound;
When Anna's sceptre points the laws their course,
And her example gives her precepts force:
There scarce is room for satire; all our lays
Must be, or songs of triumph, or of praise.
But as in grounds best cultivated, tares
And poppies rise among the golden ears;
Our product so, fit for the field or school,
Must mix with nature's favorite plant — a fool:
A weed that has to twenty summers ran,
Shoots up in stalk, and vegetates to man.
Sampling our author goes from field to field,
And culls such fools as may diversion yield;
And, thanks to Nature, there's no want of those,
For, rain or shine, the thriving coxcomb grows.
Follies tonight we show ne'er lashed before,
Yet such as nature shows you every hour;
Nor can the pictures give a just offence,
For fools are made for jests to men of sense.

---

[1] A popular actor, friend and biographer of Farquhar.
[2] William Wycherley, author of *The Plain Dealer*.

Act One

Saturday evening at the public room of the inn at Lich-field. It is a large panelled room, sparsely decorated with hunting pictures. A heavy oblong table and a few sturdy wooden chairs constitute the only furniture. Lighted candles on the table indicate that it is evening.

The play opens with the entrance from the right of the landlord Boniface, who comes puffing on in a state of great excitement. He is a big, robust, ruddy man, dressed in a brown and red waistcoat and a taproom apron.

BONIFACE: (*bellowing*) Chamberlain! Maid! Cherry! Daughter Cherry! All asleep? All dead?

His daughter Cherry comes running in from the left. Petite, pert, and pretty, she wears a saucy maid's cap perched on the back of her head and a small, frilly white muslin apron over her rather plain but attractive smock.

CHERRY: Here, here! Why d'ye bawl so, Father? D'ye think we have no ears?

BONIFACE: You deserve to have none, you young minx! The company of the Warrington coach has stood in the hall this hour, and nobody to show them to their chambers.

CHERRY: (*tossing her head*) And let 'em wait farther. There's neither red-coat in the coach nor footman behind it.

BONIFACE: But they threaten to go to another inn to-night.

CHERRY: That they dare not, for fear the coachman should overturn them tomorrow. (*calling off to the right*) Coming! Coming! — Here's the London coach arrived.

One of the right proscenium doors opens to admit several people with trunks, bandboxes, and other luggage carried by servants. They are followed by the Chamberlain, whose function is the supervision of the bedrooms and who, accordingly, carries a large steel ring of keys suspended about his waist.

BONIFACE: (*bowing*) Welcome, ladies!

CHERRY: (*archly*) Very welcome, gentlemen! Chamberlain, show the Lion and the Rose.

The Chamberlain leads the group off to the left to inspect their rooms (then denoted by names instead of numbers). Cherry follows them. Immediately after her exit, Aimwell enters through the right door, followed by his friend Archer. Aimwell wears a long blue coat, a yellow waistcoat, light drab pantaloons, boots and spurs, his three-cornered hat resting on an elaborately curled wig which is tied at the back of his neck with a ribbon and a bow. Archer, dressed in a footman's blue livery coat with shoulder-knots, the yellow collar and cuffs of his shirtwaist protruding prominently, carries a heavy portmanteau. Although both of the young men are unusually handsome and alert in appearance, they are in subtle contrast. Aimwell is to be conceived of as reserved and reticent without being colorlessly stiff and formal. ·To the contrary, his social style — elegance conscious of high breeding — produces the effect of easy and graceful naturalness. Archer (in the tradition made famous by Garrick) is a figure of easy and fascinatingly impudent assurance; he is the imperiously self-confident amorist rendered amiable by wit and invincible gaiety.

BONIFACE: (*obviously impressed, with a very low bow*) This way, this way, gentlemen!

AIMWELL: (*peremptorily, to Archer*) Set down the

BONIFACE

things; go to the stable and see my horses well rubbed.

ARCHER: I shall, sir.

He goes off to the right.

AIMWELL: You're my landlord, I suppose?

BONIFACE: (*heartily*) Yes, sir, I'm old Will Boniface, pretty well known upon this road, as the saying is.

AIMWELL: (*mockingly doffing his hat in a dignified bow*) O, Mr. Boniface, your servant!

BONIFACE: (*overwhelmed*) O, sir! What will your honor please to drink, as the saying is.

AIMWELL: I have heard your town of Lichfield much famed for ale. I think I'll taste that.

BONIFACE: (*expansively*) Sir, I have now in my cellar ten tun of the best ale in Staffordshire. 'Tis smooth as oil, sweet as milk, clear as amber, and strong as brandy; and will be just fourteen year old the fifth day of next March, old style.[1]

AIMWELL: You're very exact, I find, in the age of your ale.

BONIFACE: As punctual, sir, as I am in the age of my children. I'll show you such ale! (*calling off to the left*) Here, Tapster, broach number 1706, as the saying is. — Sir, you shall taste my *Anno Domini*. I have lived in Lichfield, man and boy, above eight-and-fifty years, and, I believe, have not consumed eight-and-fifty ounces of meat.

AIMWELL: At a meal, you mean, if one may guess your sense by your bulk.

BONIFACE: Not in my life, sir. I have fed purely upon ale; I have eat my ale, drank my ale, and I always sleep upon ale.

(*Enter Tapster with a bottle and glass, which he gives to Boniface, and then exits.*) Now, sir, you shall see!

---

[1] An error in the Julian calendar was corrected in 1582 by Pope Gregory XIII. The Gregorian calendar (new style) was gradually adapted throughout Europe but was opposed in Britain by popular prejudice. Many, like Boniface, preferred to adhere to the Julian mode (old style).

(*filling the glass and holding it up in a toast*) Your worship's health. (*drinking*) Ha! delicious, delicious! Fancy it burgundy, only fancy it, and 'tis worth ten shillings a quart.

He refills the glass and hands it to Aimwell.

AIMWELL: (*tasting it*) 'Tis confounded strong! (*He returns the glass to Boniface.*)

BONIFACE: Strong! It must be so, or how should we be strong that drink it?

AIMWELL: And have you lived so long upon this ale, Landlord?

BONIFACE: Eight-and-fifty years, upon my credit, sir; but it killed my wife, poor woman, as the saying is.

AIMWELL: How came that to pass?

BONIFACE: (*thoughtfully*) I don't know how, sir; she would not let the ale take its natural course, sir; she was for qualifying it every now and then with a dram, as the saying is; and an honest gentleman that came this way from Ireland made her a present of a dozen bottles of usquebaugh[2] — but the poor woman was never well after. But howe'er, I was obliged to the gentleman, you know.

AIMWELL: (*much amused*) Why, was it the usquebaugh that killed her?

BONIFACE: (*most seriously*) My Lady Bountiful said so. She, good lady, did what could be done; she cured her of three tympanies,[3] but the fourth carried her off. But she's happy, and I'm contented, as the saying is.

AIMWELL: (*pricking up his fortune-hunting ears at the mention of a Lady*) Who's that Lady Bountiful you mentioned?

BONIFACE: Ods my life, sir, we'll drink her health. (*drinks*) My Lady Bountiful is one of the best of women. Her last husband, Sir Charles Bountiful, left

[2] Whiskey.
[3] Inflated or distended condition of the abdomen.

her worth a thousand pound a year; and, I believe, she
lays out one half on't in charitable uses for the good
of her neighbors. She cures rheumatisms, ruptures, and
broken shins in men; green-sickness, obstructions, and
fits of the mother[4] in women; the king's evil, chin-
cough,[5] and chilblains in children: in short, she has
cured more people in and about Lichfield within ten
years than the doctors have killed in twenty; and that's
a bold word.

AIMWELL: (*much interested*) Has the lady been any
other way useful in her generation?

BONIFACE: Yes, sir; she has a daughter by Sir Charles,
the finest woman in all our country, and the greatest
fortune. She has a son too, by her first husband, Squire
Sullen, who married a fine lady from London t'other
day; if you please, sir, we'll drink his health.

AIMWELL: (*brushing aside the offer*) What sort of a
man is he?

BONIFACE: (*as if with considerable effort to describe
him*) Why, sir, the man's well enough — says little,
thinks less, and does — nothing at all, faith. (*with
quick confidence*) But he's a man of a great estate, and
values nobody.

AIMWELL: A sportsman, I suppose?

BONIFACE: (*nodding in complete agreement*) Yes, sir,
he's a man of pleasure: he plays at whisk[6] and smokes
his pipe eight-and-forty hours together sometimes.

AIMWELL: And married, you say?

BONIFACE: Ay, and to a curious woman, sir. (*again
seeming to have difficulty with his description*) — But
he's a — He wants it here, sir. (*pointing to his forehead*)

AIMWELL: (*with a slap on his purse-pocket*) He has it
there, you mean.

---

[4] Anemia, obstructions of menstrual flow, and hysteria.
[5] Scrofula and whooping-cough.
[6] Whist.

BONIFACE: That's none of my business; he's my land-lord, and so a man, you know, would not — (*flustered*) — But — ecod, he's no better than — Sir, my humble service to you. (*He drinks.*) Though I value not a far-thing what he can do to me. I pay him his rent at quar-terday; I have a good running trade; I have but one daughter, and I can give her — but no matter for that.

AIMWELL: You're very happy, Mr. Boniface. Pray, what other company have you in town?

BONIFACE: A power of fine ladies; and then we have the French officers.

AIMWELL: Oh, that's right, you have a good many of those gentlemen. Pray, how do you like their company?

BONIFACE: (*enthusiastically*) So well, as the saying is, that I could wish we had as many more of 'em; they're full of money and pay double for everything they have. They know, sir, that we paid good round taxes for the taking of 'em, and so they are willing to reimburse us a little. One of 'em lodges in my house.

Archer re-enters from the right.

ARCHER: Landlord, there are some French gentlemen below that ask for you.

BONIFACE: I'll wait on 'em. (*starting off but pausing to speak quietly to Archer*) Does your master stay long in town, as the saying is?

ARCHER: I can't tell, as the saying is.

BONIFACE: Come from London?

ARCHER: No.

BONIFACE: Going to London, mayhap?

ARCHER: No.

BONIFACE: (*aside*) An odd fellow this. (*bowing to Aimwell as he leaves*) I beg your worship's pardon; I'll wait on you in half a minute.

AIMWELL: (*after making certain that Boniface is out of hearing*) The coast's clear, I see. (*clapping Archer on the arms*) Now, my dear Archer, welcome to Lich-field!

ARCHER: I thank thee, my dear brother in iniquity.

AIMWELL: Iniquity! Prithee, leave canting; you need not change your style with your dress.

ARCHER: Don't mistake me, Aimwell, for 'tis still my maxim that there is no scandal like rags, nor any crime so shameful as poverty.

AIMWELL: The world confesses it every day in its practice, though men won't own it for their opinion. Who did that worthy lord, my brother, single out of the side-box to sup with him t'other night?

ARCHER: *(acting out the part)* Jack Handicraft, a handsome, well-dressed, mannerly, sharping rogue, who keeps the best company in town.

AIMWELL: Right! And, pray, who married my lady Manslaughter t'other day, the great fortune?

ARCHER: Why, Nick Marabone, a professed pick-pocket and good bowler; but he makes a handsome figure and rides in his coach that he formerly used to ride behind.

AIMWELL: But did you observe poor Jack Generous in the Park last week?

ARCHER: Yes, with his autumnal periwig, shading his melancholy face, his coat older than anything but its fashion, with one hand idle in his pocket, and with the other picking his useless teeth; and though the Mall was crowded with company, yet was poor Jack as single and solitary as a lion in a desert.

AIMWELL: And as much avoided, for no crime upon earth but the want[7] of money.

ARCHER: And that's enough. Men must not be poor; idleness is the root of all evil; the world's wide enough, let 'em bustle. Fortune has taken the weak under her protection, but men of sense are left to their industry.

AIMWELL: Upon which topic we proceed, and, I think, luckily hitherto. Would not any man swear now that I am a man of quality, and you my servant, when

[7] Lack.

if our intrinsic value were known —

ARCHER: Come, come, we are the men of intrinsic value who can strike our fortunes out of ourselves, whose worth is independent of accidents in life, or revolutions in government; we have heads to get money and hearts to spend it.

AIMWELL: As to our hearts, I grant ye, they are as willing tits as any within twenty degrees; but I can have no great opinion of our heads from the service they have done us hitherto, unless it be that they have brought us from London hither to Lichfield, made me a lord and you my servant.

ARCHER: That's more than you could expect already. But what money have we left?

AIMWELL: But two hundred pound.

ARCHER: And our horses, clothes, rings, etc. — Why, we have very good fortunes now for moderate people; and let me tell you, that this two hundred pound, with the experience that we are now masters of, is a better estate than the ten we have spent. Our friends, indeed, began to suspect that our pockets were low; but we came off with flying colors, showed no signs of want either in word or deed.

AIMWELL: Ay, and our going to Brussels was a good pretence enough for our sudden disappearing; and, I warrant you, our friends imagine that we are gone a-volunteering.

ARCHER: (*glum only for a moment at the prospect of enlisting*) Why, faith, if this prospect fails, it must e'en come to that. (*recovering*) I am for venturing one of the hundreds, if you will, upon this knight-errantry; but in case it should fail, we'll reserve t'other to carry us to some counterscarp,[8] where we may die, as we lived, in a blaze.

---

[8] The opposite side of a ditch around a fort. The implied proposal is to use the other hundred to procure commissions for themselves.

AIMWELL: With all my heart; and we have lived justly, Archer. We can't say that we have spent our fortunes, but that we have enjoyed 'em.

ARCHER: Right! So much pleasure for so much money, we have had our pennyworths; and, had I millions, I would go to the same market again. — O London, London! — Well, we have had our share, and let us be thankful. Past pleasures, for aught I know, are best, such as we are sure of; those to come may disappoint us.

AIMWELL: It has often grieved the heart of me to see how some inhuman wretches murder their kind fortunes; those that, by sacrificing all to one appetite, shall starve all the rest. — You shall have some that live only in their palates, and in their sense of tasting shall drown the other four. Others are only epicures in appearances, such who shall starve their nights to make a figure a-days, and famish their own to feed the eyes of others. A contrary sort confine their pleasures to the dark, and contract their spacious acres to the circuit of a muff-string.

ARCHER: Right! But they find the Indies in that spot where they consume 'em, and I think your kind keepers[9] have much the best on 't; for they indulge the most senses by one expense. There's the seeing, hearing, and feeling, amply gratified; and some philosophers will tell you that from such a commerce there arises a sixth sense that gives infinitely more pleasure than the other five put together.

AIMWELL: And to pass to the other extremity, of all keepers I think those the worst that keep their money.

ARCHER: Those are the most miserable wights in being; they destroy the rights of nature and disappoint the blessings of Providence. Give me a man that keeps

---

[9] Keepers of mistresses.

ARCHER

his five senses keen and bright as his sword, that has 'em always drawn out in their just order and strength, with his reason as commander at the head of 'em; that detaches 'em by turns upon whatever party of pleasure agreeably offers, and commands 'em to retreat upon the least appearance of disadvantage or danger! For my part, I can stick to my bottle while my wine, my company, and my reason hold good; I can be charmed with Sappho's singing without falling in love with her face; I love hunting, but would not, like Actaeon,[10] be eaten up by my own dogs; I love a fine house, but let another keep it; and just so I love a fine woman.

AIMWELL: (*with a wry smile of self-confession*) In that last particular you have the better of me.

ARCHER: Ay, you're such an amorous puppy that I'm afraid you'll spoil our sport; you can't counterfeit the passion without feeling it.

AIMWELL: Though the whining part be out of doors[11] in town, 'tis still in force with the country ladies; and let me tell you, Frank, the fool in that passion shall outdo the knave at any time.[12]

ARCHER: Well, I won't dispute it now; you command for the day, and so I submit. — At Nottingham, you know, I am to be master.

AIMWELL: And at Lincoln, I again.

ARCHER: Then, at Norwich I mount, which, I think, shall be our last stage; for, if we fail there, we'll embark for Holland, bid adieu to Venus, and welcome Mars.

AIMWELL: A match! (*Seeing Boniface about to enter from the left, he puts a finger to his lips*) Mum!

---

[10] The huntsman in classical mythology who, having surprised Diana while bathing, was changed into a stag and devoured by his own dogs.

[11] Out of fashion.

[12] The joker, in cards, will beat the jack.

BONIFACE: (*coming in and addressing them in his usual unctious fashion*) What will your worship please to have for supper?

AIMWELL: What have you got?

BONIFACE: Sir, we have a delicate piece of beef in the pot, and a pig at the fire.

AIMWELL: Good supper-meat, I must confess. — I can't eat beef, landlord.

ARCHER: And I hate pig.

AIMWELL: (*in mock anger at his servant's effrontery*) Hold your prating, sirrah! Do you know who you are?

BONIFACE: Please to bespeak something else; I have everything in the house.

AIMWELL: Have you any veal?

BONIFACE: Veal! Sir, we had a delicate loin of veal on Wednesday last.

AIMWELL: Have you got any fish or wildfowl?

BONIFACE: As for fish, truly, sir, we are an inland town, and indifferently provided with fish, that's the truth on 't; and then for wildfowl — we have a delicate couple of rabbits.

AIMWELL: (*in an off-handed manner as if settling the matter*) Get me the rabbits fricasseed.

BONIFACE: Fricasseed! Lard, sir, they'll eat much better smothered with onions.

ARCHER: Pshaw! Damn your onions!

AIMWELL: (*sternly, to Archer*) Again, sirrah! — Well, landlord, what you please. But hold, I have a small charge of money, and your house is so full of strangers that I believe it may be safer in your custody than mine; for when this fellow of mine gets drunk, he minds nothing. (*to Archer*) Here, sirrah, reach me the strong-box.

ARCHER: Yes, sir. (*aside*) This will give us a reputation. (*He opens the portmanteau and extracts the strong-box.*)

AIMWELL: (*taking the box and handing it to Boni-*

face) Here, landlord; the locks are sealed down both for your security and mine; it holds somewhat above two hundred pound; if you doubt it, I'll count it to you after supper; but be sure you lay it where I may have it at a minute's warning; for my affairs are a little dubious at present. Perhaps I may be gone in half an hour; perhaps I may be your guest till the best part of that be spent; and pray order your ostler to keep my horses always saddled. But one thing above the rest I must beg, that you would let this fellow have none of your *Anno Domini*, as you call it; for he's the most insufferable sot. (*to Archer*) Here, sirrah, light me to my chamber.

With a scarcely perceptible grimace, Archer picks a candlestick from the table and lights his master off to their room, the downstage (front) left proscenium door.

BONIFACE: (*calling*) Cherry! Daughter Cherry!

CHERRY: (*entering from the right*) D'ye call, father?

BONIFACE: Ay, child, you must lay by this box for the gentleman; 'tis full of money.

CHERRY: (*taking the box and exhibiting surprise at its weight*) Money! All that money! Why, sure, father, the gentleman comes to be chosen parliament-man. Who is he?

BONIFACE: I don't know what to make of him. He talks of keeping his horses ready saddled, and of going perhaps at a minute's warning, or of staying perhaps till the best part of this be spent.

CHERRY: Ay, ten to one, father, he's a highwayman.

BONIFACE: A highwayman! Upon my life, girl, you have hit it, and this box is some new-purchased booty. (*struck by a sudden thought*) Now, could we find him out, the money were ours.

CHERRY: He don't belong to our gang.

BONIFACE: What horses have they?

CHERRY: The master rides upon a black.

BONIFACE: A black! Ten to one the man upon the black mare; and since he don't belong to our fraternity, we may betray him with a safe conscience. I don't think it lawful to harbor any rogues but my own. — Look ye, child, as the saying is, we must go cunningly to work; proofs we must have. The gentleman's servant loves drink, I'll ply him that way; and ten to one loves a wench, — you must work him t'other way.

CHERRY: (*as if shocked*) Father, would you have me give my secret for his?

BONIFACE: Consider, child, there's two hundred pound to boot. (*ringing without*) Coming! Coming! — Child, mind your business. (*He goes off to right.*)

CHERRY: (*angrily*) What a rogue is my father! My father? I deny it. — My mother was a good, generous, free-hearted woman, and I can't tell how far her good nature might have extended for the good of her children. This landlord of mine, for I think I can call him no more, would betray his guest and debauch his daughter into the bargain, — by a footman, too!

Re-enter Archer.

ARCHER: What footman, pray, mistress, is so happy as to be the subject of your contemplation.

CHERRY: (*brusquely*) Whoever he is, friend, he'll be but little the better for't.

ARCHER: I hope so, for I'm sure you did not think of me.

CHERRY: Suppose I had?

ARCHER: (*ingratiatingly*) Why, then you're but even with me; for the minute I came in, I was a-considering in what manner I should make love to you.

CHERRY: (*as if surprised*) Love to me, friend!

ARCHER: (*attempting to embrace her*) Yes, child.

CHERRY: (*pushing him away*) Child! Manners! — If you kept a little more distance, friend, it would become you much better.

ARCHER: (*with easy disdain*) Distance! Good-night, sauce-box. (*He makes as if to leave.*)

CHERRY: (*aside*) A pretty fellow! I like his pride. (*to

Archer) Sir, pray, sir, you see sir — (*Archer returns.*)
I have the credit to be entrusted with your master's
fortune here, which sets me a degree above his footman.
(*coyly*) I hope, sir, you an't affronted?

ARCHER: (*taking her face between his hands*) Let me
look you full in the face, and I'll tell you whether you
can affront me or no. — 'Sdeath, child, you have a pair
of delicate eyes and you don't know what to do with
'em!

CHERRY: (*with exaggerated ingenuousness*) Why, sir,
don't I see everybody?

ARCHER: Ay, but if some women had 'em, they would
kill everybody. — Prithee, instruct me, I would fain
make love to you, but I don't know what to say.

CHERRY: Why, did you never make love to anybody
before?

ARCHER: (*releasing her and stepping back as if to
admire her figure*) Never to a person of your figure, I
can assure you, madam. My addresses have been always confined to people within my own sphere; I never
aspired so high before. (*singing*)

> But you look so bright,
> And are dressed so tight,
> That a man would swear you're right,
>   As arm was e'er laid over.
> Such an air
> You freely wear
> To ensnare,
>   As makes each guest a lover!

> Since then, my dear, I'm your guest,
> Prithee give me of the best,
> Of what is ready drest.

CHERRY: (*aside*) What can I think of this man? (*to
Archer*) Will you give me that song, sir?

ARCHER: Ay, my dear, take it while 'tis warm. (*He
kisses her.*) Death and fire! Her lips are honeycombs.

CHERRY

Keogh

CHERRY: And I wish there had been bees too, to have stung you for your impudence.

ARCHER: There's a swarm of Cupids, my little Venus, that has done the business much better.

CHERRY: (*aside*) This fellow is misbegotten as well as I. (*to Archer*) What's your name, sir?

ARCHER: (*aside*) Name! egad, I have forgot it. (*to Cherry*) Oh! Martin.

CHERRY: Where were you born?

ARCHER: In St. Martin's parish.

CHERRY: What was your father?

ARCHER: St. Martin's parish.

CHERRY: (*stepping back*) Then, friend, good-night.

ARCHER: (*pursuing*) I hope not.

CHERRY: You may depend upon 't.

ARCHER: Upon what?

CHERRY: That you're very impudent.

ARCHER: That you're very handsome.

CHERRY: That you're a footman.

ARCHER: That you're an angel. (*He takes her hand to stop her continued retreat.*)

CHERRY: (*raising her other hand as if contemplating slapping him*) I shall be rude.

ARCHER: (*as if to kiss her again*) So shall I.

CHERRY: Let go my hand.

ARCHER: Give me a kiss. (*As he kisses her, Boniface calls from outside:* Cherry! Cherry!)

CHERRY: I'm-m — my father calls; you plaguy devil, how durst you stop my breath so? — Offer to follow me one step, if you dare. (*She goes off to the right.*)

ARCHER: (*in high delight*) A fair challenge, by this light! This is a pretty fair opening of an adventure; but we are knight-errants, and so Fortune be our guide. (*He goes off to the left.*)

Act Two

*The next morning. A "gallery," or enclosed promenade
for walking in bad weather, in Lady Bountiful's house.
Ancestral portraits or other paintings might adorn the
back wall. Mrs. Sullen and Dorinda enter from opposite
sides and meet. Mrs. Sullen is a handsome, sprightly
woman who outshines her pretty but quieter sister-in-
law both in costume and in bearing. Both women are
beautifully and elaborately dressed in the billowing,
frilly, frothy lace and chiffon fashions of the day, foamy
and diaphanous, but they differ as does the scent of
fresh roses from that of a fragrant, exotic perfume.
Dorinda is gentle and innocent, inexperienced and art-
less. But she is in no wise limply insipid. Rather her
dominant mood is one of romantic high spirits. Mrs.
Sullen, however, is fundamentally a figure of pathos:
Beauty married to the Beast. She is a sophisticated London lady of pleasure-loving, sensuous temperament
turned sultry through boredom and continual thwart-
ing. She is now light and charming, now frantic and
exasperated. She is full of feminine wiles: caprice and
compunctions, flutterings of the heart, agitations of the
soul; now languid and yearning and languishing, now
satiric, ironic, or bitter. On this churchgoing morning,
her smart petite hat is tipped rakishly to the right side
of her head and slightly over her right eye, revealing an
elegant left profile. Her quintessential femininity is
accented by a cluster of bright ribbons gaily pendant
from the hat and ringlets of hair worn at the right side
of the neck.*

DORINDA: Morrow, my dear sister; are you for church this morning?

MRS. SULLEN: (*exasperated*) Anywhere to pray; for Heaven alone can help me. But I think, Dorinda, there's no form of prayer in the liturgy against bad husbands.

DORINDA: (*sympathetically*) But there's a form of law in Doctors-Commons[1]; and I swear, sister Sullen, rather than see you thus continually discontented, I would advise you to apply to that: for besides the part that I bear in your vexatious broils, as being sister to the husband and friend to the wife, your example gives me such an impression of matrimony that I shall be apt to condemn my person to a long vacation all its life. — (*meditating for a moment*) But supposing, madam, that you brought it to a case of separation, what can you urge against your husband? My brother is, first, the most constant man alive.

MRS. SULLEN: (*with a sigh of resignation*) The most constant husband, I grant ye.

DORINDA: He never sleeps from you.

MRS. SULLEN: No, he always sleeps with me.

DORINDA: He allows you a maintenance suitable to your quality.

MRS. SULLEN: (*spiritedly*) A maintenance! Do you take me, madam, for an hospital child,[2] that I must sit down and bless my benefactors for meat, drink, and clothes? As I take it, madam, I brought your brother ten thousand pounds, out of which I might expect some pretty things, called pleasures.

DORINDA: (*reasonably*) You share in all the pleasures that the country affords.

---

[1] A college for professors of law where matrimonial courts were held.

[2] A pauper raised in one of the charitable institutions known as "hospitals."

*Will you be pleased, my dear, to drink tea
with us this morning?*

MRS. SULLEN: Country pleasures! Racks and torments! Dost think, child, that my limbs were made for leaping of ditches and clamb'ring over stiles? Or that my parents, wisely foreseeing my future happiness in country pleasures, had early instructed me in rural accomplishments of drinking fat ale, playing at whisk, and smoking tobacco with my husband? Or of spreading of plasters, brewing of diet-drinks, and stilling rosemary-water, with the good old gentlewoman, my mother-in-law?

DORINDA: I'm sorry, madam, that it is not more in our power to divert you. I could wish, indeed, that our entertainments were a little more polite, or your taste a little less refined. But, pray, madam, how came the poets and philosophers, that labored so much in hunting after pleasure, to place it at last in a country life?

MRS. SULLEN: Because they wanted money, child, to find out the pleasures of the town. Did you ever see a poet or philosopher worth ten thousand pound? If you can show me such a man, I'll lay you fifty pound you'll find him somewhere within the weekly bills.[3] — Not that I disapprove rural pleasures, as the poets have painted them; in their landscape, every Phyllis has her Corydon,[4] every murmuring stream, and every flow'ry mead, gives fresh alarms to love.— Besides, you'll find that their couples were never married. (*catching sight of her husband slowly approaching offstage right*) But yonder I see my Corydon, and a sweet swain it is, Heaven knows! Come, Dorinda, don't be angry, he's my husband, and your brother; and, between both, is he not a sad brute?

DORINDA: I have nothing to say to your part of him, — you're the best judge.

MRS. SULLEN: (*exploding*) O sister, sister! if ever you marry, beware of a sullen, silent sot, one that's always

---

[3] The Weekly Bills recorded births and deaths in London.

[4] Shepherdess and shepherd in Vergil's *Eclogues*.

musing, but never thinks. — There's some diversion in a talking blockhead; and since a woman must wear chains, I would have the pleasure of hearing 'em rattle a little. — Now you shall see, but take this by the way. — He came home this morning at his usual hour of four, wakened me out of a sweet dream of something else by tumbling over the tea-table, which he broke all to pieces; after his man and he had rolled about the room, like sick passengers in a storm, he comes flounce into bed, dead as a salmon into a fishmonger's basket; his feet cold as ice, his breath hot as a furnace, and his hands and his face as greasy as his flannel night-cap. — O matrimony! — He tosses up the clothes with a barbarous swing over his shoulders, disorders the whole economy of my bed, leaves me half naked, and my whole night's comfort is the tuneable serenade of that wakeful nightingale, his nose! — Oh, the pleasure of counting the melancholy clock by a snoring husband! — But now, sister, you shall see how handsomely, being a well-bred man, he will beg my pardon.

Sullen enters slowly from the right, in morning gown and dressing cap. Beefy and florid, he is a torrid, torpid, besotted, paunchy John Bull of the eighteenth-century squirearchy.

SULLEN: *(holding his head)* My head aches consumedly.

MRS. SULLEN: *(gently and with exaggerated solicitude)* Will you be pleased, my dear, to drink tea with us this morning? It may do your head good.

SULLEN: No.

DORINDA: Coffee, brother?

SULLEN: Pshaw!

MRS. SULLEN: Will you please to dress, and go to church with me? The air may help you.

SULLEN: *(bellowing hoarsely)* Scrub!

Scrub, his manservant, enters from the right. An appropriate valet for his doltish master, he is lumpish and sloppily dressed in a light blue livery coat trimmed with red and yellow lace, red breeches, a long white cravat with square ends, and a long, rather messy blue apron.

SCRUB: (*in a colorless voice*) Sir.

SULLEN: What day o' th' week is this?

SCRUB: (*thoughtfully*) Sunday, an't please your worship.

SULLEN: Sunday! Bring me a dram; and d'ye hear, set out the venison-pasty, and a tankard of strong beer upon the hall-table; I'll go to breakfast. (*He starts off to the left.*)

DORINDA: Stay, stay, brother, you shan't get off so; you were very naughty last night and must make your wife reparation. Come, come, brother, won't you ask pardon?

SULLEN: (*dully*) For what?

DORINDA: For being drunk last night.

SULLEN: I can afford it, can't I?

MRS. SULLEN: (*sharply*) But I can't, sir.

SULLEN: Then you may let it alone.

MRS. SULLEN: But I must tell you, sir, that this is not to be borne.

SULLEN: I'm glad on't.

MRS. SULLEN: (*between anger and entreaty*) What is the reason, sir, that you use me thus inhumanly?

SULLEN: Scrub!

SCRUB: Sir.

SULLEN: Get things ready to shave my head. (*He turns abruptly and goes off to the right.*)

MRS. SULLEN: (*to Scrub as he follows Sullen off*) Have a care of coming near his temples, Scrub, for fear you meet something there that may turn the edge of your razor. (*to Dorinda*) Inveterate stupidity! Did you ever know so hard, so obstinate a spleen as his? O sister, sister! I shall never ha' good of the beast till I get him to town: London, dear London, is the place for managing and breaking a husband.

DORINDA: And has not a husband the same opportunities there for humbling a wife?

MRS. SULLEN: No, no, child, 'tis a standing maxim in conjugal discipline, that when a man would enslave his wife, he hurries her into the country; and when a lady would be arbitrary with her husband, she wheedles her booby up to town. — A man dare not play the tyrant in London, because there are so many examples to encourage the subject to rebel. O Dorinda, Dorinda! a fine woman may do anything in London: o' my conscience, she may raise an army of forty thousand men.

DORINDA: (*with a meaningful smile*) I fancy, sister, you have a mind to be trying your power that way here in Lichfield; you have drawn the French count to your colors already.

MRS. SULLEN: (*offhandedly*) The French are a people that can't live without their gallantries.

DORINDA: (*pointedly*) And some English that I know, sister, are not averse to such amusements.

MRS. SULLEN: (*laughing*) Well, sister, since the truth must out, it may do as well now as hereafter; I think one way to rouse my lethargic, sottish husband is to give him a rival. Security begets negligence in all people, and men must be alarmed to make 'em alert in their duty. Women are like pictures, of no value in the hands of a fool till he hears men of sense bid high for the purchase.

DORINDA: (*seriously*) This might do, sister, if my brother's understanding were to be convinced into a passion for you; but I fancy there's a natural aversion on his side; and I fancy, sister, that you don't come much behind him, if you dealt fairly.

MRS. SULLEN: I own it, we are united contradictions, fire and water. But I could be contented, with a great many other wives, to humor the censorious mob, and give the world an appearance of living well with my husband, could I bring him but to dissemble a little kindness to keep me in countenance.

DORINDA: But how do you know, sister, but that, instead of rousing your husband by this artifice to counterfeit kindness, he should awake in a real fury?

MRS. SULLEN: (*with light insouciance*) Let him: if I can't entice him to the one, I would provoke him to the other.

DORINDA: (*showing real concern*) But how must I behave myself between ye?

MRS. SULLEN: You must assist me.

DORINDA: What, against my own brother!

MRS. SULLEN: (*with buoyant confidence*) He's but half a brother, and I'm your entire friend. If I go a step beyond the bounds of honor, leave me; till then, I expect you should go along with me in everything; while I trust my honor in your hands, you may trust your brother's in mine. — The count is to dine here today.

DORINDA: 'Tis a strange thing, sister, that I can't like that man.

MRS. SULLEN: You like nothing; your time is not come. Love and death have their fatalities, and strike home one time or other. — You'll pay for all one day, I warrant ye. — But come, my lady's tea is ready, and 'tis almost church time.

She encircles Dorinda's waist in warm friendliness, and they go off to the left.

SCENE TWO

The public room at the Inn on the same morning. Aimwell and Archer enter from their room at the left. Aimwell is magnificently attired: opera hat, full dress blue coat, gilt buttons, white waistcoat and breeches, silk stockings, pumps and buckles. Archer is in shirt-sleeves as if he had just finished assisting in his "master's" toilet.

AIMWELL: *(amused)* And was she the daughter of the house?

ARCHER: The landlord is so blind as to think so; but I dare swear she has better blood in her veins.

AIMWELL: Why dost think so?

ARCHER: Because the baggage has a pert *je ne sais quoi;* she reads plays, keeps a monkey, and is troubled with vapors.[5]

AIMWELL: By which discoveries I guess that you know more of her.

ARCHER: Not yet, faith; the lady gives herself airs; forsooth, nothing under a gentleman!

AIMWELL: *(with kindly condescension)* Let me take her in hand.

ARCHER: *(sharply)* Say one word more o' that, and I'll declare myself, spoil your sport there, and everywhere else; look ye, Aimwell, every man in his own sphere.

AIMWELL: Right, and therefore you must pimp for your master.

ARCHER: *(bowing)* In the usual forms, good sir, after I have served myself. — But to our business. — You are so well dressed, Tom, and make so handsome a figure, that I fancy you may do execution in a country church; the exterior part strikes first, and you're in the right to make that impression favorable.

AIMWELL: There's something in that which may turn to advantage. The appearance of a stranger in a country church draws as many gazers as a blazing-star; no sooner he comes into the cathedral, but a train of whispers runs buzzing round the congregation in a moment: Who is he? Whence comes he? Do you know him? — Then I, sir, tips me the verger with half a crown; he pockets the simony, and inducts me into the best pew in the church. I pull out my snuff-box, turn myself

---

[5] An ailment of fashionable ladies: melancholy or the blues.

round, bow to the bishop, or the dean, if he be the commanding officer; single out a beauty, rivet both my eyes to hers, set my nose a-bleeding by the strength of imagination, and show the whole church my concern by my endeavoring to hide it. After the sermon, the whole town gives me to her for a lover, and by persuading the lady that I am a-dying for her, the tables are turned, and she in good earnest falls in love with me.

ARCHER: (*drily*) There's nothing in this, Tom, without a precedent; but instead of riveting your eyes to a beauty, try to fix 'em upon a fortune; that's our business at present.

AIMWELL: Pshaw! No woman can be a beauty without a fortune. Let me alone, for I am a marksman.

ARCHER: (*as if struck by a sudden thought*) Tom!

AIMWELL: Ay.

ARCHER: When were you at church before, pray?

AIMWELL: Um — I was there at the coronation.[6]

ARCHER: And how can you expect a blessing by going to church now?

AIMWELL: Blessing! Nay, Frank, I ask but for a wife.

With a flourish, he goes off through a right proscenium door.

ARCHER: (*returning to his chamber*) Truly, the man is not very unreasonable in his demands.

Boniface enters from the right wings in conversation with Cherry.

BONIFACE: Well, daughter, as the saying is, have you brought Martin to confess?

CHERRY: Pray, father, don't put me upon getting anything out of a man; I'm but young, you know, father, and I don't understand wheedling.

BONIFACE: Young! Why, you jade, as the saying is, can any woman wheedle that is not young? Your mother

---

[6] The first performance of the play was nearly five years after the coronation of Queen Anne on April 23, 1702.

was useless at five-and-twenty. Not wheedle! Would you make your mother a whore and me a cuckold, as the saying is? I tell you his silence confesses it, and his master spends his money so freely, and is so much a gentleman.every manner of way, that he must be a highwayman.

Gibbet, an evil-looking highwayman, wearing faded regimentals and shrouded in a black cloak, enters stealthily by the right door. A black patch over one eye accentuates the general effect of a pirate-parody costume.

GIBBET: (*in a stage-whisper*) Landlord, landlord, is the coast clear?

BONIFACE: (*easily*) O Mr. Gibbet, what's the news?

GIBBET: No matter, ask no questions, all fair and honorable. — Here, my dear Cherry. (*producing . a money-bag from under his cloak and giving it to her*) Two hundred sterling pounds, as good as any that ever hanged or saved a rogue; lay 'em by with the rest; and here — three wedding or mourning rings, 'tis much the same, you know. — (*continuing to produce articles from inside pouches*) Here, two silver-hilted swords; I took those from fellows that never show any part of their swords but the hilts. Here is a diamond necklace which the lady hid in the privatest place in the coach, but I found it out. This gold watch I took from a pawnbroker's wife; it was left in her hands by a person of quality — there's the arms upon the case.

CHERRY: But who had you the money from?

GIBBET: (*with mock-sadness*) Ah! poor woman! I pitied her; — from a poor lady just eloped from her husband. She had made up her cargo and was bound for Ireland as hard as she could drive; she told me of her husband's barbarous usage, and so I left her half a crown. (*reaching inside the cloak again*) But I had almost forgot, my dear Cherry, I have a present for you.

CHERRY: What is 't?

GIBBET: (*producing a small cosmetic jar*) A pot of ceruse, my child, that I took out of a lady's under-pocket.

CHERRY: What! Mr. Gibbet, do you think that I paint?

GIBBET: Why, you jade, your betters do; I'm sure the lady that I took it from had a coronet upon her handkerchief. — Here, take my cloak, and go, secure the premises.

CHERRY: I will secure 'em.

She goes off to the right, loaded with the booty.

BONIFACE: But, hark ye, where's Hounslow and Bagshot?

GIBBET: They'll be here tonight.

BONIFACE: D'ye know of any other gentlemen o' the pad [7] on this road?

GIBBET: No.

BONIFACE: I fancy that I have two that lodge in the house just now.

GIBBET: The devil! How d'ye smoke 'em?

BONIFACE: Why, the one is gone to church.

GIBBET: (*pondering*) That's suspicious, I must confess.

BONIFACE: And the other is now in his master's chamber; he pretends to be servant to the other. We'll call him out and pump him a little.

GIBBET: With all my heart.

BONIFACE: (*calling off to left*) Mr. Martin! Mr. Martin.

Enter Archer combing a periwig and singing.

GIBBET: (*to Boniface*) The roads are consumed deep; I'm as dirty as Old Brentford [8] at Christmas. — A good pretty fellow that. (*to Archer*) Whose servant are you, friend?

ARCHER: My master's.

---

[7] Highway robbers.

[8] A town about eight miles west of London.

GIBBET: Really!

ARCHER: Really.

GIBBET: That's much. — The fellow has been at the bar by his evasions. — But pray, sir, what is your master's name?

ARCHER: (*singing and seemingly rapt in the combing of the periwig*) *Tall, all dall!* — This is the most obstinate curl —

GIBBET: I ask you his name.

ARCHER: Name, sir — *tall, all dall!* — I never asked him his name in my life. — *Tall, all dall!*

BONIFACE: (*aside to Gibbet*) What think you now?

GIBBET: (*aside to Boniface*) Plain, plain; he talks now as if he were before a judge. (*to Archer*) But pray, friend, which way does your master travel?

ARCHER: A-horseback.

GIBBET: (*aside*) Very well again, an old offender, right. (*to Archer*) But I mean, does he go upwards or downwards?

ARCHER: Downwards, I fear, sir. — *Tall, all!*

GIBBET: (*ruefully*) I'm afraid my fate will be a contrary way.

BONIFACE: Ha, ha, ha! Mr. Martin, you're very arch. — This gentleman is only travelling towards Chester, and would be glad of your company, that's all. — Come, Captain, you'll stay tonight, I suppose? I'll show you a chamber. — Come, Captain.

GIBBET: (*to Archer*) Farewell, friend.

ARCHER: (*with a slightly exaggerated bow*) Captain, your servant. (*Boniface and Gibbet go off to the left.*) Captain! A pretty fellow! 'Sdeath, I wonder that the officers of the army don't conspire to beat all scoundrels in red but their own.

Cherry enters quietly through a right back wing. Seeing Archer alone, she stops.

CHERRY: (*aside*) Gone! and Martin here! I hope he did not listen; I would have the merit of the discovery all my own, because I would oblige him to love me. (*coming forward*) Mr. Martin, who was that man with my father?

ARCHER: (*turning*) Some recruiting sergeant, or whipped-out trooper, I suppose.

CHERRY: (*aside*) All's safe, I find.

ARCHER: (*moving toward her*) Come, my dear, have you conned over the catechism I taught you last night?

CHERRY: (*archly*) Come, question me.

ARCHER: (*assuming the role of a schoolmaster*) What is love?

CHERRY: (*as if reciting*) Love is I know not what, it comes I know not how, and goes I know not when.

ARCHER: Very well, an apt scholar. (*He chucks her under the chin.*) Where does love enter?

CHERRY: Into the eyes.

ARCHER: And where go out?

CHERRY: (*demurely*) I won't tell ye.

ARCHER: What are the objects of that passion?

CHERRY: Youth, beauty, and clean linen.

ARCHER: The reason?

CHERRY: The two first are fashionable in nature, and the third at court.

ARCHER: That's my dear. — What are the signs and tokens of that passion?

CHERRY: A stealing look, a stammering tongue, words improbable, designs impossible, and actions impracticable.

ARCHER: That's my good child, kiss me. (*He kisses her.*) What must a lover do to obtain his mistress?

CHERRY: He must adore the person that disdains him, he must bribe the chambermaid that betrays him, and court the footman that laughs at him. — He must — he must —

ARCHER: (*with mock severity*) Nay, child, I must whip you if you don't mind your lesson; he must treat his —

CHERRY: Oh, ay! — He must treat his enemies with

And then shall we go make the bed?

respect, his friends with indifference, and all the world with contempt; he must suffer much and fear more; he must desire much and hope little; in short, he must embrace his ruin, and throw himself away.

ARCHER: (*delighted*) Had ever man so hopeful a pupil as mine! — Come, my dear, why is love called a riddle?

CHERRY: Because, being blind, he leads those that see, and, though a child, he governs a man.

ARCHER: Mighty well! — And why is Love pictured blind?

CHERRY: Because the painters out of the weakness or privilege of their art chose to hide those eyes that they could not draw.

ARCHER: That's my dear little scholar, kiss me again. (*She obliges.*) And why should Love, that's a child, govern a man?

CHERRY: Because that a child is the end of love.

ARCHER: And so ends Love's catechism. (*putting his arm around her waist*) And now, my dear, we'll go in and make my master's bed.

CHERRY: Hold, hold, Mr. Martin! — You have taken a great deal of pains to instruct me, and what d'ye think I have learned by it?

ARCHER: What?

CHERRY: That your discourse and your habit[9] are contradictions, and·it would be nonsense in me to believe you a footman any longer.

ARCHER: Oons,[10] what a witch it is!

CHERRY: (*very seriously*) Depend upon this, sir, nothing in this garb shall ever tempt me; for, though I was born to servitude, I hate it. — Own your condition, swear you love me, and then —

ARCHER: And then we shall go make the bed?

CHERRY: Yes.

---

[9] Dress; his footman's livery.
[10] A emphemism for "God's Wounds."

ARCHER: (*releasing and facing her*) You must know, then, that I am born a gentleman, my education was liberal; but I went to London a younger brother, fell into the hands of sharpers, who stripped me of my money; my friends disowned me, and now my necessity brings me to what you see.

CHERRY: Then take my hand — promise to marry me before you sleep, and I'll make you master of two thousand pound.

ARCHER: How?

CHERRY: Two thousand pound that I have this minute in my own custody; so, throw off your livery this instant, and I'll go find a parson.

ARCHER: What said you? A parson!

CHERRY: What! do you scruple?

ARCHER: Scruple! No, no, but — Two thousand pound, you say?

CHERRY: And better.

ARCHER: (*aside*) 'Sdeath, what shall I do? (*to Cherry*) But hark'ee, child, what need you make me master of yourself and money, when you may have the same pleasure out of me, and still keep your fortune in your hands?

CHERRY: (*stepping back*) Then you won't marry me?

ARCHER: (*embarrassed and confused*) I would marry you, but —

CHERRY: (*with a merry laugh*) O sweet sir, I'm your humble servant; you're fairly caught! Would you persuade me that any gentleman who could bear the scandal of wearing a livery would refuse two thousand pound, let the condition be what it would? — No, no, sir. — But I hope you'll pardon the freedom I have taken, since it was only to inform myself of the respect that I ought to pay you. (*After a mock curtsey she starts off to the right.*)

ARCHER: (*aside*) Fairly bit, by Jupiter! (*aloud*) Hold! Hold! — And have you actually two thousand pound?

CHERRY: Sir, I have my secrets as well as you; when you please to be more open, I shall be more free, and be assured that I have discoveries that will match yours, be what they will. In the meanwhile, be satisfied that no discovery I make shall ever hurt you; but beware of my father! (*She goes off.*)

ARCHER: (*musing aloud*) So! We're like to have as many adventures in our inn as Don Quixote had in his. Let me see — two thousand pound! — If the wench would promise to die when the money were spent, egad, one would marry her; but the fortune may go off in a year or two, and the wife may live — Lord knows how long. Then an innkeeper's daughter! Ay, that's the devil — there my pride brings me off.

> For whatsoe'er the sages charge on pride,
> The angels' fall, and twenty faults beside,
> On earth, I'm sure, 'mong us of mortal calling,
> Pride saves man oft, and woman too, from falling.

He retires to his chamber.

Act Three

The Gallery in Lady Bountiful's house. Mrs. Sullen and Dorinda have just returned from church and come in together from the left.

MRS. SULLEN: (*in high good humor*) Ha, ha, ha! my dear sister, let me embrace thee! Now we are friends indeed; for I shall have a secret of yours as a pledge for mine. — Now you'll be good for something; I shall have you conversable in the subjects of the sex.

DORINDA: (*disdainfully but rather weakly*) But do you think that I am so weak as to fall in love with a fellow at first sight?

MRS. SULLEN: Pshaw! Now you spoil all; why should not we be as free in our friendships as the men? I warrant you the gentleman has got to his confidant already, has avowed his passion, toasted your health, called you ten thousand angels, has run over your lips, eyes, neck, shape, air, and everything, in a description that warms their mirth to a second enjoyment.

DORINDA: Your hand, sister, I an't well.

MRS. SULLEN: So — she's breeding already! — Come, child, up with it — hem a little — so — now tell me, don't you like the gentleman that we saw at church just now.

DORINDA: (*faintly*) The man's well enough.

MRS. SULLEN: Well enough! Is he not a demigod, a Narcissus, a star, the man i' the moon?

DORINDA: (*wilting*) O sister, I'm extremely ill!

MRS. SULLEN: Shall I send to your mother, child, for

a little of her cephalic plaster[1] to put to the soles of your feet, or shall I send to the gentleman for something for you? — Come, unlace your stays, unbosom yourself. — The man is perfectly a pretty fellow; I saw him when he first came into church.

DORINDA: (*starry-eyed*) I saw him too, sister, and with an air that shone, methought, like rays about his person.

MRS. SULLEN: Well said, up with it!

DORINDA: (*warming to her subject and becoming increasingly animated as she continues*) No forward coquette behavior, no airs to set him off, no studied looks nor artful posture — but Nature did it all —

MRS. SULLEN: Better and better! — One touch more — come!

DORINDA: But then his looks — did you observe his eyes?

MRS. SULLEN: Yes, yes, I did. — His eyes, well, what of his eyes?

DORINDA: (*dreamily*) Sprightly, but not wandering; they seemed to view, but never gazed on anything but me. — And then his looks so humble were, and yet so noble, that they aimed to tell me that he could with pride die at my feet, though he scorned slavery anywhere else.

MRS. SULLEN: The physic works purely! — How d'ye find yourself now, my dear?

DORINDA: (*blushing*) Hem! Much better, my dear. (*looking off to the left*) Oh, here comes our Mercury! (*Enter Scrub.*) Well, Scrub, what news of the gentleman?

SCRUB: (*solemnly*) Madam, I have brought you a packet of news.

DORINDA: Open it quickly, come.

SCRUB: (*counting off his points on his fingers*) In the first place I inquired who the gentleman was; they told me he was a stranger. Secondly, I asked what the gentle-

---

[1] For relieving pains in the head.

man was; they answered and said that they never saw him before. Thirdly, I inquired what countryman he was; they replied, 'twas more than they knew. Fourthly, I demanded whence he came; their answer was, they could not tell. And fifthly, I asked whither he went; and they replied, they knew nothing of the matter, — and this is all I could learn.

MRS. SULLEN: (*with a trace of exasperation*) But what do the people say? Can't they guess?

SCRUB: Why, some think he's a spy, some guess he's a mountebank, some say one thing, some another; but for my part, I believe he's a Jesuit.

DORINDA: A Jesuit! Why a Jesuit?

SCRUB: Because he keeps his horses always ready saddled, and his footman talks French.

MRS. SULLEN: His footman!

SCRUB: Ay, he and the count's footman were jabbering French like two intriguing ducks in a mill-pond; and I believe they talked of me, for they laughed consumedly.

DORINDA: What sort of livery has the footman?

SCRUB: Livery! Lord, madam, I took him for a captain, he's so bedizened with lace. And then he has tops to his shoes, up to his mid leg, a silver-headed cane dangling at his knuckles; he carries his hands in his pockets just so — (*He walks in the French air*) — and has a fine long periwig tied up in a bag. — Lord, madam, he's clear another sort of man than I.

MRS. SULLEN: (*drily*) That may easily be. — But what shall we do now, sister?

DORINDA: I have it. — This fellow has a world of simplicity, and some cunning; the first hides the latter by abundance. — Scrub!

SCRUB: Madam!

DORINDA: We have a great mind to know who this gentleman is, only for our satisfaction.

SCRUB: Yes, madam, it would be a satisfaction, no doubt.

DORINDA: You must go and get acquainted with his footman, and invite him hither to drink a bottle of your ale, because you're butler today.

SCRUB: Yes, madam, I am butler every Sunday.

MRS. SULLEN: O brave, sister! O' my conscience, you understand the mathematics already. 'Tis the best plot in the world: your mother, you know, will be gone to church, my spouse will be got to the alehouse with his scoundrels, and the house will be our own — so we drop in by accident and ask the fellow some questions ourselves. In the country, you know, any stranger is company, and we're glad to take up with the butler in a country-dance, and happy if he'll do us the favor.

Enter Gipsy, the maid, from the left.

GIPSY: Ladies, dinner's upon table. (*She retires.*)

DORINDA: Scrub, we'll excuse your waiting — go where we ordered you.

SCRUB: I shall.

He goes off to the right. Mrs. Sullen and Dorinda follow the maid, left.

SCENE TWO

Back at the Inn. The time of this scene is simultaneous with the preceding one: soon after church. Aimwell and Archer enter from the left.

ARCHER: Well, Tom, I find you're a marksman.

AIMWELL: (*in high fettle*) A marksman! Who so blind could be as not discern a swan among the ravens?

ARCHER: Well, but hark'ee, Aimwell—

AIMWELL: Aimwell! Call me Oroondates. Caesario, Amadis,[2] all that romance can in a lover paint, and

---

[2] Oroondates was the king of Scythia in La Calpranede's romance *Cassandra*; also in *The Rival Kings* by John Banks. Caesario was the name assumed by Viola in Shakespeare's *Twelfth Night*. Amadis de Gaul was the hero of the romance by that name, by Vasco de Lobeira.

then I'll answer. O Archer! I read her thousands in her looks; she looked like Ceres[3] in her harvest: corn, wine, and oil, milk and honey, gardens, groves, and purling streams played on her plenteous face

ARCHER: Her face! Her pocket, you mean; the corn, wine, and oil lies there. In short, she has ten thousand pound, that's the English on 't.

AIMWELL: Her eyes —

ARCHER: Are demi-cannons, to be sure; so I won't stand their battery. (*He starts off to the left as if bored and disgusted.*)

AIMWELL: (*checking his ardor*) Pray excuse me, my passion must have vent.

ARCHER: (*pausing*) Passion! What a plague d'ye think these romantic airs will do our business? Were my temper as extravagant as yours, my adventures would have something more romantic by half.

AIMWELL: (*scornfully*) Your adventures!

ARCHER: (*imitating Aimwell's previously exalted manner*) Yes:

> The nymph that with her twice ten hundred
>   pounds,
> With brazen engine hot, and quoif [4] clear starched,
> Can fire the guest in warming of the bed —

There's a touch of sublime Milton for you, and the subject but an innkeeper's daughter! I can play with a girl as an angler does with his fish; he keeps it at the end of his line, runs it up the stream and down the stream, till at last he brings it to hand, tickles the trout, and so whips it into his basket.

Boniface enters from the right.

BONIFACE: Mr. Martin, as the saying is — Yonder's an honest fellow below, my Lady Bountiful's butler,

---

[3] The Greek goddess of fertility.
[4] A close-fitting cap worn by women.

who begs the honor that you would go home with him
and see his cellar.

ARCHER: Do my *baise-mains*[5] to the gentleman, and
tell him I will do myself the honor to wait on him
immediately.

Boniface retires.

AIMWELL: (*back to his previous state of transport —
but now mocking*) What do I hear?

Soft Orpheus play, and fair Toftida sing! [6]

ARCHER: Pshaw! Damn your raptures! I tell you, here's
a pump going to be put into the vessel, and the ship
will get into harbor, my life on't. You say there's another lady very handsome there?

AIMWELL: Yes, faith.

ARCHER: I am in love with her already.

AIMWELL: Can't you give me a bill upon Cherry in
the meantime?

ARCHER: (*emphatically*) No, no, friend, all her corn,
wine, and oil is ingrossed to my market. — And once
more I warn you to keep your anchorage clear of mine;
for if you fall foul of me, by this light you shall go to
the bottom! — What! Make a prize of my little frigate,
while I am upon the cruise for you! —

AIMWELL: (*placatingly*) Well, well, I won't. — (*Archer
nods and goes off to his chamber. Boniface re-enters from
the right.*) Landlord, have you any tolerable company
in the house? I don't care for dining alone.

BONIFACE: Yes, sir. There's a captain below, as the
saying is, that arrived about an hour ago.

AIMWELL: Gentlemen of his coat are welcome everywhere. Will you make him a compliment from me, and
tell him I should be glad of his company?

---

[5] Hand-kissing.

[6] Mrs. Katherine Tofts, the leading soprano of England in the
reign of Queen Anne, to be accompanied by Orpheus, the supreme musician of Greek mythology.

BONIFACE: (*shrewdly*) Who shall I tell him, sir, would —

AIMWELL: Ha! That stroke was well thrown in! — I'm only a traveller like himself, and would be glad of his company, that's all.

BONIFACE: (*attempting to conceal his chagrin*) I obey your commands, as the saying is.

He bows faintly and goes off to the right, just as Archer reappears at the left.

ARCHER: (*in a state of perturbation*) 'Sdeath! I had forgot. What title will you give yourself?

AIMWELL: (*calmly*) My brother's, to be sure; he would never give me anything else, so I'll make bold with his honor this bout, — You know the rest of your cue.

ARCHER: (*retiring*) Ay, ay.

Gibbet wanders in from the right.

GIBBET: (*with an elaborate bow*) Sir, I'm yours.

AIMWELL: (*brusquely*) 'Tis more than I deserve, sir, for I don't know you.

GIBBET: I don't wonder at that, sir, for you never saw me before — (*aside*) I hope.

AIMWELL: And pray, sir, how came I by the honor of seeing you now?

GIBBET: Sir, I scorn to intrude upon any gentleman — but my landlord —

AIMWELL: O, sir, I ask you pardon! You're the captain he told me of?

GIBBET: At your service, sir.

AIMWELL: What regiment, may I be so bold?

GIBBET: A marching regiment, sir, an old corps.

AIMWELL: (*aside*) Very old, if your coat be regimental. — (*aloud*) You have served abroad, sir?

GIBBET: (*broadly*) Yes, sir — in the plantations; 'twas my lot to be sent into the worst service. I would have quitted it indeed, but a man of honor, you know — Besides, 'twas for the good of my country that I should be abroad. — Anything for the good of one's country. — I'm a Roman for that.

AIMWELL: (*aside*) One of the first, I'll lay my life. — (*aloud*) You found the West Indies very hot, sir?

GIBBET: Ay, sir, too hot for me.

AIMWELL: Pray, sir, han't I seen your face at Will's coffee-house? [7]

GIBBET: Yes, sir, and at White's,[8] too.

AIMWELL: And where is your company now, captain?

GIBBET: They an't come yet.

AIMWELL: Why, d'ye expect 'em here?

GIBBET: They'll be here tonight, sir.

AIMWELL: Which way do they march?

GIBBET: Across the country. — (*aside*) The devil's in't, if I han't said enough to encourage him to declare! But I'm afraid he's not right; I must tack about.

AIMWELL: Is your company to quarter in Lichfield?

GIBBET: In this house, sir.

AIMWELL: What! All?

GIBBET: My company's but thin, ha, ha, ha! We are but three, ha, ha, ha!

AIMWELL: You're merry, sir.

GIBBET: Ay, sir, you must excuse me, sir; I understand the world, especially the art of travelling; I don't care, sir, for answering questions directly upon the road — for I generally ride with a charge about me.

AIMWELL: (*aside*) Three or four, I believe.

GIBBET: I am credibly informed that there are highwaymen upon this quarter; not, sir, that I could suspect a gentleman of your figure — but truly, sir, I have got such a way of evasion upon the road that I don't care for speaking truth to any man.

AIMWELL: Your caution may be necessary. — Then I presume you're no captain?

---

[7] One of the best known of London coffee houses, noted for its patronage by outstanding literary men.

[8] Nearly as famous as Will's; Swift and Steele were among its frequenters.

GIBBET: Not I, sir; captain is a good travelling name, and so I take it. It stops a great many foolish inquiries that are generally made about gentlemen that travel; it gives a man an air of something, and makes the drawers[9] obedient: — and thus far I am a captain, and no farther.

AIMWELL: And pray, sir, what is your true profession?

GIBBET: O sir, you must excuse me! — Upon my word, sir, I don't think it safe to tell you.

AIMWELL: (*as Boniface reappears at the right*) Ha, ha, ha! Upon my word, I commend you. Well, Mr. Boniface, what's the news?

BONIFACE: There's another gentleman below, as the saying is, that hearing you were but two, would be glad to make the third man, if you would give him leave.

AIMWELL: What is he?

BONIFACE: A clergyman, as the saying is.

AIMWELL: A clergyman! Is he really a clergyman? or is it only his travelling name, as my friend the captain has it?

BONIFACE: O sir, he's a priest, and chaplain to the French officers in town.

AIMWELL: Is he a Frenchman?

BONIFACE: Yes, sir, born at Brussels.

GIBBET: A Frenchman and a priest! I won't be seen in his company, sir; I have a value for my reputation, sir.

AIMWELL: (*persuasively*) Nay, but, captain, since we are by ourselves — Can he speak English, landlord?

BONIFACE: Very well, sir; you may know him, as the saying is, to be a foreigner by his accent, and that's all.

AIMWELL: Then he has been in England before?

BONIFACE: Never, sir; but he's a master of languages, as the saying is. He talks Latin — it does me good to hear him talk Latin.

AIMWELL: Then you understand Latin, Mr. Boniface?

---

[9] Drawers of liquor; loosely, bartenders.

BONIFACE: Not I, sir, as the saying is; but he talks it so very fast that I'm sure it must be good.

AIMWELL: Pray, desire him to walk up.

BONIFACE: Here he is, as the saying is.

Foigard enters from the right. He is a tall, thin, rather ungainly and very Irish-looking priest. He is dressed in black and wears a silver cross suspended by a chain around his neck.

FOIGARD: (*enthusiastically*) Save you, gentlemens, both.

AIMWELL: (*aside*) A Frenchman! — (*bowing to Foigard*) Sir, your most humble servant.

FOIGARD: (*as if transported with delight*) Och, dear joy,[10] I am your most faithful shervant, and yours alsho.

GIBBET: (*suspiciously*) Doctor, you talk very good English, but you have a mighty twang of the foreigner.

FOIGARD: My English is very vel for the vords, but we foreigners, you know, cannot bring our tongues about the pronunciation so soon.

AIMWELL: (*aside*) A foreigner! a downright Teague,[11] by this light. (*aloud*) Were you born in France, doctor?

FOIGARD: I was educated in France, but I was borned at Brussels; I am a subject of the King of Spain, joy.

GIBBET: (*sharply*) What King of Spain, sir? Speak!

FOIGARD: (*vaguely*) Upon my shoul, joy, I cannot tell you as yet.

AIMWELL: Nay, captain, that was too hard upon the doctor; he's a stranger.

FOIGARD: Oh, let him alone, dear joy; I am of a nation that is not easily put out of countenance.

AIMWELL: Come, gentlemen, I'll end the dispute. — Here, landlord, is dinner ready yet?

BONIFACE: (*with a sweeping gesture toward the left*) Upon the table, as the saying is.

---

[10] A well-known Irish expression.

[11] A generic term for Irishmen.

AIMWELL: (*indicating one of the left proscenium doors*) Gentlemen — pray — that door —

FOIGARD: (*holding back*) No, no, fait, the captain must lead.

AIMWELL: (*bowing*) No, doctor, the church is our guide.

GIBBET: Ay, ay, so it is.

Foigard, obviously flattered, leads the way out, followed by Aimwell and Gibbet.

SCENE THREE

A room in Lady Bountiful's house. A handsome marble fireplace with a large painting of Venus over its mantle is centered at the back so that it dominates the room and gives an impression of elegance further enhanced by two other large paintings on either side of the back wall. The painting at the left is modelled on Lebrun's "Battles of Alexander," created for Louis XIV. At the right is a Correggio-like painting of the conquest of Leda by Jupiter disguised as a swan. Smaller paintings are interspersed, among them a head of Ovid at the right, a portrait of Mrs. Sullen hung over a handsome cabinet at the left, and a painting of Salmoneus being struck by lightning by Zeus for his effrontery in attempting to imitate the god's thunderbolts. (These paintings become important in Act IV.) A table and chairs are placed at the right of the fireplace and considerably forward.

It is early evening of the same day. From the left Archer and Scrub stagger in, singing and hugging one another. Archer is now elaborately dressed in a scarlet uniform coat, white breeches, silk stockings, and pumps with buckles; blue and silver gilt showing at the neck and sleeves. Scrub tipsily waves a tankard with one hand. Archer is obviously not as drunk as he pretends. They are followed at a discreet distance by Gipsy who is carefully observing their behavior.

SCRUB: Tall, all dall! — Come, my dear boy, let's have that song once more.

ARCHER: No, no, we shall disturb the family. — But will you be sure to keep the secret?

SCRUB: Pho! upon my honor, as I'm a gentleman.

ARCHER: 'Tis enough. — You must know, then, that my master is the Lord Viscount Aimwell; he fought a duel t'other day in London, wounded his man so dangerously that he thinks fit to withdraw till he hears whether the gentleman's wounds be mortal or not. He never was in this part of England before, so he chose to retire to this place, that's all.

GIPSY: (*aside*) And that's enough for me.

She ducks offstage.

SCRUB: And where were you when your master fought?

ARCHER: We never know of our masters' quarrels.

SCRUB: No? If our masters in the country here receive a challenge, the first thing they do is to tell their wives; the wife tells the servants, the servants alarm the tenants, and in half an hour you shall have the whole county in arms.

ARCHER: To hinder two men from doing what they have no mind for. — But if you should chance to talk now of my business?

SCRUB: Talk! Ay, sir, had I not learned the knack of holding my tongue, I had never lived so long in a great family.

ARCHER: (*with seeming casualness*) Ay, ay, to be sure there are secrets in all families.

SCRUB: Secrets! Ay — but I'll say no more. Come, sit down, we'll make an end of our tankard: here —

He gives Archer the tankard and drops into one of the chairs.

ARCHER: With all my heart; who knows but you and I may come to be better acquainted, eh? (*holding up the tankard*) Here's your ladies' healths; you have three, I think, and to be sure there must be secrets among 'em. (*He drinks, puts the tankard on the table, draws a chair close to Scrub's and sits down beside him.*)

SCRUB: Secrets! Ay, friend. — I wish I had a friend —

ARCHER: (*throwing an arm about his shoulders*) Am I not your friend? Come, you and I will be sworn brothers.

SCRUB: (*rather soddenly*) Shall we?

ARCHER: From this minute. — Give me a kiss. (*He leans over and kisses Scrub on the cheek.*) And now, brother Scrub —

SCRUB: (*intimately*) And now, brother Martin, I will tell you a secret that will make your hair stand on end. — You must know that I am consumedly in love.

ARCHER: (*wryly*) That's a terrible secret, that's the truth on 't.

SCRUB: That jade, Gipsy, that was with us just now in the cellar, is the arrantest whore that ever wore a petticoat; and I'm dying for love of her.

ARCHER: Ha, ha, ha! — Are you in love with her person or her virtue, brother Scrub?

SCRUB: I should like virtue best, because it is more durable than beauty; for virtue holds good with some women long, and many a day after they have lost it.

ARCHER: In the country, I grant ye, where no woman's virtue is lost till a bastard be found.

SCRUB: Ay, could I bring her to a bastard, I should have her all to myself; but I dare not put it upon that lay, for fear of being sent for a soldier. — Pray, brother, how do you gentlemen in London like that same Pressing Act? [12]

ARCHER: Very ill, brother Scrub; 'tis the worst that ever was made for us. Formerly I remember the good days when we could dun our masters for our wages, and if they refused to pay us, we could have a warrant to carry 'em before a Justice; but now if we talk of eating,

---

[12] The Impressment Acts made it possible to impress indigent men into military service.

they have a warrant for us, and carry us before three Justices.

SCRUB: And to be sure we go, if we talk of eating; for the Justices won't give their own servants a bad example. Now this is my misfortune — I dare not speak in the house, while that jade Gipsy dings about like a fury. — Once I had the better end of the staff.

ARCHER: And how comes the change now?

SCRUB: Why, the mother of all this mischief is a priest.

ARCHER: A priest!

SCRUB: Ay, a damned son of a whore of Babylon, that came over hither to say grace to the French officers and eat up our provisions. — There's not a day goes over his head without a dinner or supper in this house.

ARCHER: How came he so familiar in the family?

SCRUB: Because he speaks English as if he had lived here all his life, and tells lies as if he had been a traveller from his cradle.

ARCHER: And this priest, I'm afraid, has converted the affections of your Gipsy.

SCRUB: (*vehemently*) Converted! Ay, and perverted, my dear friend: for I'm afraid he has made her a whore and a papist! — But this is not all; there's the French count and Mrs. Sullen, they're in the confederacy, and for some private ends of their own, to be sure.

ARCHER: A very hopeful family yours, brother Scrub! I suppose the maiden lady has her lover too?

SCRUB: (*thoughtfully*) Not that I know. She's the best on 'em, that's the truth on't. But they take care to prevent my curiosity by giving me so much business that I'm a perfect slave. — What d'ye think is my place in this family?

ARCHER: Butler, I suppose.

SCRUB: Ah, Lord help you! — I'll tell you. — Of a Monday I drive the coach; of a Tuesday I drive the plough; on Wednesday I follow the hounds; a-Thursday I dun the tenants; on Friday I go to market; on Saturday I draw warrants; and a-Sunday I draw beer.

ARCHER: Ha, ha, ha! If variety be a pleasure in life, you have enough on't, my dear brother. (*observing Mrs. Sullen and Dorinda about to enter from the right*) But what ladies are those?

SCRUB: (*peering in their direction*) Ours, ours; that upon the right hand is Mrs. Sullen, and the other is Mistress Dorinda. — Don't mind 'em; sit still, man.

Archer, who had begun to rise, sits back in his chair as the ladies stroll slowly across the stage as if engaged in a private conversation and seemingly oblivious of the servants.

MRS. SULLEN: I have heard my brother talk of my Lord Aimwell; but they say that his brother is the finer gentleman.

DORINDA: That's impossible, sister.

They pause at the left — now quite remote from the servants at the right.

MRS. SULLEN: He's vastly rich, but very close, they say.

DORINDA: No matter for that; if I can creep into his heart, I'll open his breast, I warrant him. (*in a lowered voice*) I have heard say that people may be guessed at by the behavior of their servants; I could wish we might talk to that fellow.

MRS. SULLEN: (*sotto voce*) So do I; for I think he's a very pretty fellow. Come this way; I'll throw out a lure for him presently.

They turn and move slowly toward the right.

ARCHER: (*aside*) Corn, wine, and oil indeed! — But, I think, the wife has the greatest plenty of flesh and blood; she should be my choice. (*Mrs. Sullen drops her glove.*) Ah, a, say you so! (*Archer jumps up, retrieves the glove and restores it to Mrs. Sullen with a gallant bow*) Madam — your ladyship's glove.

MRS. SULLEN: O sir, I thank you! — (*to Dorinda*) What a handsome bow the fellow has.

DORINDA: Bow! Why, I have known several footmen come down from London set up here for dancing-masters, and carry off the best fortunes in the country.

ARCHER: (*aside*) That project, for aught I know, had been better than ours. (*to Scrub*) Brother Scrub, why don't you introduce me?

SCRUB: (*pulling himself together and rising clumsily*) Ladies, this is the strange gentleman's servant that you saw a church today. I understood he came from London, and so I invited him to the cellar that he might show me the newest flourish in whetting my knives.

DORINDA: (*graciously*) And I hope you have made much of him?

ARCHER: Oh yes, madam, but the strength of your ladyship's liquor is a little too potent for the constitution of your humble servant.

MRS. SULLEN: What, then you don't usually drink ale?

ARCHER: (*delicately*) No, madam; my constant drink is tea, or a little wine and water. 'Tis prescribed me by the physician for a remedy against the spleen.

SCRUB: O la! O la! A footman have the spleen!

MRS. SULLEN: I thought that distemper had been only proper to people of quality.

ARCHER: Madam, like all other fashions it wears out and so descends to their servants; though in a great many of us, I believe, it proceeds from some melancholy particles in the blood, occasioned by the stagnation of wages.

DORINDA: (*aside to Mrs. Sullen*) How affectedly the fellow talks! — (*to Archer*) How long, pray, have you served your present master?

ARCHER: Not long; my life has been mostly spent in the service of the ladies.

MRS. SULLEN: And pray, which service do you like best?

ARCHER: (*gallantly*) Madam, the ladies pay best: the honor of serving them is sufficient wages; there is a charm in their looks that delivers a pleasure with their

My life has been mostly spent in the service of the ladies.

commands, and gives our duty the wings of inclination.

MRS. SULLEN: (*aside*) That flight was above the pitch of a livery. (*to Archer*) And, sir, would not you be satisfied to serve a lady again?

ARCHER: As a groom of the chamber, madam, but not as a footman.

MRS. SULLEN: I suppose you served as footman before?

ARCHER: For that reason I would not serve in that post again; for my memory is too weak for the load of messages that the ladies lay upon their servants in London. My Lady Howd'ye, the last mistress I served, called me up one morning, and told me, "Martin, go to my Lady Allnight with my humble service; tell her I was to wait on her ladyship yesterday, and left word with Mrs. Rebecca that the preliminaries of the affair she knows of are stopped till we know the concurrence of the person that I know of, for which there are circumstances wanting which we shall accommodate at the old place; but that in the meantime there is a person about her ladyship that, from several hints and surmises, was accessory at a certain time to the disappointments that naturally attend things that to her knowledge are of more importance — "

MRS. SULLEN, DORINDA: (*interrupting this Niagara of words*) Ha! ha! ha! Where are you going, sir?

ARCHER: Why, I han't half done! — The whole howd'ye was about half an hour long; so I happened to misplace two syllables, and was turned off and rendered incapable.

DORINDA: (*aside to Mrs. Sullen*) The pleasantest fellow, sister, I ever saw! (*to Archer*) But, friend, if your master be married, I presume you still serve a lady?

ARCHER: No, madam, I take care never to come into a married family; the commands of the master and mistress are always so contrary that 'tis impossible to please both.

DORINDA: (aside) There's a main point gained: my lord is not married, I find.

MRS. SULLEN: But I wonder, friend, that in so many good services you had not a better provision made for you.

ARCHER: I don't know how, madam. I had a lieutenancy offered me three or four times; but that is not bread, madam — I live much better as I do.

SCRUB: Madam, he sings rarely! I was thought to do pretty well here in the country till he came; but alack a day, I'm nothing to my brother Martin!

DORINDA: Does he? — Pray, sir, will you oblige us with a song?

ARCHER: Are you for passion or humor?

SCRUB: Oh le! He has the purest ballad about a trifle —

MRS. SULLEN: A trifle! Pray, sir, let's have it.

ARCHER: (modestly) I'm ashamed to offer you a trifle, madam; but since you command me —

He sings to the tune of "Sir Simon the King." [13]

> A trifling song you shall hear,
> Begun with a trifle and ended:
> All trifling people draw near,
> And I shall be nobly attended.
>
> Were it not for trifles, a few
> That lately have come into play;
> The men would want something to do,
> And the women want something to say.
>
> What makes men trifle in dressing?
> Because the ladies (they know)
> Admire, by often possessing,
> That eminent trifle, a beau.

---

[13] A popular song alluding to Simon Wadlow, host of the Devil Tavern in the early seventeenth century.

When the lover his moments has trifled,
The trifle of trifles to gain;
No sooner the virgin is rifled
But a trifle shall part 'em again.

What mortal man would be able
At White's half an hour to sit?
Or who could bear a tea-table
Without talking of trifles for wit?

The court is from trifles secure,
Gold keys are no trifles, we see:
White rods are no trifles, I'm sure,
Whatever their bearers may be.

But if you will go to the place
Where trifles abundantly breed,
The levee will show you His Grace
Makes promises trifles indeed.

A coach with six footmen behind
I count neither trifle nor sin:
But, ye gods! how oft do we find
A scandalous trifle within.

A flask of champagne, people think it
A trifle, or something as bad:
But if you'll contrive how to drink it,
You'll find it no trifle, egad!

A parson's a trifle at sea,
A widow's a trifle in sorrow:
A peace is a trifle today;
Who knows what may happen tomorrow!

A black coat a trifle may cloak,
Or to hide it the red may endeavor:
But if once the army is broke,
We shall have more trifles than ever.

The stage is a trifle, they say;
The reason, pray carry along,
Because at every new play
The house they with trifles so throng.

But with people's malice to trifle,
And to set us all on a foot:
The author of this is a trifle,
And his song is a trifle to boot.

MRS. SULLEN: *(delighted)* Very well, sir, we're obliged to you. *(offering him money)* Something for a pair of gloves.

ARCHER: *(bowing)* I humbly beg leave to be excused. My master, madam, pays me; nor dare I take money from any other hand without injuring his honor and disobeying his commands.

Archer and Scrub go off to the left.

DORINDA: This is surprising! Did you ever see so pretty a well-bred fellow?

MRS. SULLEN: The devil take him for wearing that livery!

DORINDA: I fancy, sister, he may be some gentleman, a friend of my lord's, that his lordship has pitched upon for his courage, fidelity, and discretion to bear him company in this dress, and who, ten to one, was his second too.

MRS. SULLEN: *(with abrupt emphasis)* It is so, it must be so, and it shall be so! — for I like him.

DORINDA: What! Better than the Count?

MRS. SULLEN: The Count happened to be the most agreeable man upon the place; and so I chose him to serve me in my design upon my husband. But I should like this fellow better in a design upon myself.

DORINDA: *(with frank impatience)* But now, sister, for an interview with this lord and this gentleman; how shall we bring that about?

MRS. SULLEN: *(with dry practicality)* Patience! You country ladies give no quarter if once you be entered. Would you prevent their desires, and give the fellows no wishing-time? Look'ee, Dorinda, if my Lord Aimwell loves you or deserves you, he'll find a way to see you, and there we must leave it. My business comes now upon the tapis.[14] Have you prepared your brother?

DORINDA: Yes, yes.

MRS. SULLEN: And how did he relish it?

DORINDA: He said little, mumbled something to himself, promised to be guided by me — but here he comes.

Squire Sullen enters from the right, now dressed: brown coat, leather breeches, boots.

SQUIRE SULLEN: (*irritably*) What singing was that I heard just now?

MRS. SULLEN: (*in honeyed accents*) The singing in your head, my dear; you complained of it all day.

SQUIRE SULLEN: (*sharply*) You're impertinent.

MRS. SULLEN: (*in the same mocking tone*) I was ever so since I became one flesh with you.

SQUIRE SULLEN: (*in a sour voice*) One flesh! Rather two carcasses joined unnaturally together.

MRS. SULLEN: Or rather a living soul coupled to a dead body.

DORINDA: So, this is fine encouragement for me!

SQUIRE SULLEN: Yes, my wife shows you what you must do.

MRS. SULLEN: And my husband shows you what you must suffer.

SQUIRE SULLEN: (*exploding*) 'Sdeath, why can't you be silent?

MRS. SULLEN: (*with equal venom*) 'Sdeath, why can't you talk?

SQUIRE SULLEN: Do you talk to any purpose?

MRS. SULLEN: Do you think to any purpose?

SQUIRE SULLEN: (*moving close to Dorinda*) Sister, hark'ee! (*whispering in her ear*) I shan't be home till it be late.

He goes abruptly off to the left.

MRS. SULLEN: What did he whisper to ye?

---

[14] Tapistry, floor-covering. "Comes now upon the tapis" is idiomatic for "is now to be considered."

DORINDA: That he would go round the back way, come into the closet, and listen as I directed him. But let me beg you once more, dear sister, to drop this project; for as I told you before, instead of awaking him to kindness, you may provoke him to a rage; and then who knows how far his brutality may carry him?

MRS. SULLEN: I'm provided to receive him, I warrant you. But here comes the Count: vanish! (*Dorinda goes quickly off to right as Count Bellair, in French dress uniform complete with cockade, enters at the left. Everything about the Count suggests the quintessence of French gallantry.*) Don't you wonder, Monsieur le Count, that I was not at church this afternoon?

COUNT BELLAIR: (*bowing and kissing her hand*) I more wonder, madam, that you go dere at all, or how you dare to lift those eyes to Heaven that are guilty of so much killing.

MRS. SULLEN: If Heaven, sir, has given to my eyes with the power of killing the virtue of making a cure, I hope the one may atone for the other.

COUNT BELLAIR: Oh, largely, madam, would your ladyship be as ready to apply the remedy as to give the wound. Consider, madam, I am doubly a prisoner; first to the arms of your general, then to your more conquering eyes. My first chains are easy — there a ransom may redeem me; but from your fetters I never shall get free.

MRS. SULLEN: (*sighing deeply*) Alas, sir! Why should you complain to me of your captivity, who am in chains myself? You know, sir, that I am bound, nay, must be tied up in that particular that might give you ease: I am like you, a prisoner of war — of war, indeed — I have given my parole of honor! Would you break yours to gain your liberty?

COUNT BELLAIR: Most certainly I would, were I a prisoner among the Turks. Dis is your case; you're a slave, madam, slave to the worst of Turks, a husband.

MRS. SULLEN: (*faintly, as if weakening*) There lies my foible, I confess; no fortifications, no courage, conduct, nor vigilancy can pretend to defend a place where the cruelty of the governor forces the garrison to mutiny.

COUNT BELLAIR: (*passionately*) And where de besieger is resolved to die before de place. (*kneeling*) Here will I fix — with tears, vows, and prayers assault your heart and never rise till you surrender; or if I must storm — (*rising*) Love and St. Michael! — (*attempting to embrace her*) And so I begin the attack.

MRS. SULLEN: (*pushing him away*) Stand off! (*aside*) Sure he hears me not! — And I could almost wish — he did not! — The fellow makes love very prettily. (*aloud*) But, sir, why should you put such a value upon my person when you see it despised by one that knows it so much better?

COUNT BELLAIR: (*taking her hand*) He knows it not, though he possesses it; if he but knew the value of the jewel he is master of, he would always wear it next his heart and sleep with it in his arms.

MRS. SULLEN: (*in seemingly tentative surrender*) But since he throws me unregarded from him —

COUNT BELLAIR: And one that knows your value well comes by and takes you up, is it not justice?

He attempts to sweep her into his arms. Squire Sullen bursts in from the right with his sword drawn.

SQUIRE SULLEN: Hold, villain, hold!

The Count releases Mrs. Sullen who wheels around, suddenly produces a pistol, and points it at her husband.

MRS. SULLEN: (*with calm, forceful definitiveness*) Do you hold!

SQUIRE SULLEN: What! Murder your husband to defend your bully!

MRS. SULLEN: (*disdainfully*) Bully! For shame, Mr. Sullen. Bullies wear long swords; the gentleman has none; he's a prisoner, you know. I was aware of your outrage and prepared this to receive your violence; and, if occasion were, to preserve myself against the force of this other gentleman.

COUNT BELLAIR: (*unperturbed by any of this*) O madam, your eyes be bettre firearms than your pistol; they nevre miss.

SQUIRE SULLEN: (*in white fury*) What! Court my wife to my face!

MRS. SULLEN: (*coldly*) Pray, Mr. Sullen, put up; suspend your fury for a minute.

SQUIRE SULLEN: To give you time to invent an excuse!

MRS. SULLEN: I need none.

SQUIRE SULLEN: No, for I heard every syllable of your discourse.

COUNT BELLAIR: Ah! and begar, I tink the dialogue was vera pretty.

MRS. SULLEN: Then I suppose, sir, you heard something of your own barbarity?

SQUIRE SULLEN: Barbarity! 'oons, what does the woman call barbarity? Do I ever meddle with you?

MRS. SULLEN: No.

SQUIRE SULLEN: As for you, sir, I shall take another time.

COUNT BELLAIR: Ah, begar, and so must I.

SQUIRE SULLEN: Look'ee, madam, don't think that my anger proceeds from any concern I have for your honor, but for my own, and if you can contrive any way of being a whore without making me a cuckold, do it and welcome.

MRS. SULLEN: Sir, I thank you kindly; you would allow me the sin but rob me of the pleasure. No, no, I'm resolved never to venture upon the crime without the satisfaction of seeing you punished for 't.

SQUIRE SULLEN: Then will you grant me this, my dear? Let anybody else do you the favor but the Frenchman, for I mortally hate his whole generation.

He turns and exits abruptly to the right.

COUNT BELLAIR: Ah, sir, that be ungrateful, for, begar, I love some of yours. (*approaching her*) Madam —

MRS. SULLEN: (*stepping back*) No, sir.

COUNT BELLAIR: (*amused*) No, sir! Garzoon, madam, I am not your husband.

MRS. SULLEN: 'Tis time to undeceive you, sir. I believed your addresses to me were no more than an amusement, and I hope you will think the same of my complaisance; and to convince you that you ought, you must know that I brought you hither only to make you instrumental in setting me right with my husband, for he was planted to listen by my appointment.

COUNT BELLAIR: By your appointment?

MRS. SULLEN: Certainly.

COUNT BELLAIR: And so, madam, while I was telling twenty stories to part you from your husband, begar, I was bringing you together all the while?

MRS. SULLEN: I ask your pardon, sir, but I hope this will give you a taste of the virtue of the English ladies.

COUNT BELLAIR: Begar, madam, your virtue be vera great, but garzoon, your honeste be vera little.

Dorinda re-enters from the right.

MRS. SULLEN: Nay, now, you're angry, sir.

COUNT BELLAIR: Angry! — *Fair Dorinda* (*He sings "Fair Dorinda," the opera tune,*[15] *and addresses Dorinda.*) Madam, when your ladyship want a fool, send for me. *Fair Dorinda, Revenge, etc.*

He goes off to the left, singing.

MRS. SULLEN: (*admiringly*) There goes the true humor of his nation — resentment with good manners and the height of anger in a song! Well, sister, you must be judge, for you have heard the trial.

DORINDA: And I bring in my brother guilty.

---

[15] A song in an operatic version of Dryden and Davenant's *Tempest* in which Dorinda was added by Dryden as a sister to Miranda.

MRS. SULLEN: (*sighing*) But I must bear the punishment. 'Tis hard, sister.

DORINDA: (*gently*) I own it; but you must have patience.

MRS. SULLEN: (*vehemently*) Patience! The cant of custom — (*quoting in a childish voice*) Providence sends no evil without remedy. (*tensely*) Should I lie groaning under a yoke I can shake off, I were accessory to my ruin, and my patience were no better than self-murder.

DORINDA: But how can you shake off the yoke? Your divisions don't come within the reach of the law for a divorce.

MRS. SULLEN: Law! What law can search into the remote abyss of nature? What evidence can prove the unaccountable disaffections of wedlock? Can a jury sum up the endless aversions that are rooted in our souls, or can a bench give judgment upon antipathies?

DORINDA: They never pretended, sister; they never meddle but in cases of uncleanness.

MRS. SULLEN: (*with deep feeling*) Uncleanness! O sister! Casual violation is a transient injury and may possibly be repaired, but can radical hatreds be ever reconciled? No, no, sister, nature is the first lawgiver, and when she has set tempers opposite, not all the golden links of wedlock nor iron manacles of law can keep 'em fast.

> Wedlock we own ordained by Heaven's decree,
> But such as Heaven Ordained it first to be —
> Concurring tempers in the man and wife
> As mutual helps to draw the load of life.
> View all the works of Providence above,
> The stars with harmony and concord move;
> View all the works of Providence below,
> The fire, the water, earth and air, we know,
> All in one plant agree to make it grow.
> Must man, the chiefest work of art divine,

Be doomed in endless discord to repine?
No, we should injure Heaven by that surmise,
Omnipotence is just, were man but wise.

*Dorinda puts her arm affectionately around Mrs.
Sullen's waist and they go off together to the right.*

SULLEN

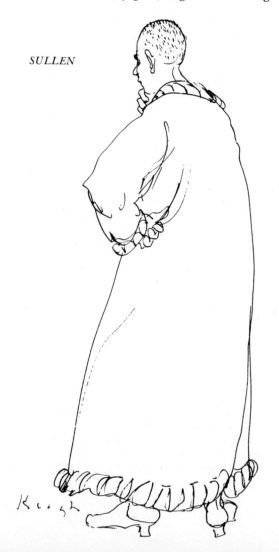

Act Four

The same room in Lady Bountiful's house. Candles are lighted to indicate the lapse of an hour or so since the preceding evening scene. Mrs. Sullen is discovered alone in the room, thoughtfully walking about and musing aloud.

MRS. SULLEN: Were I born an humble Turk, where women have no soul nor property, there I must sit contented. But in England, a country whose women are its glory, must women be abused? Where women rule, must women be enslaved? Nay, cheated into slavery, mocked by a promise of comfortable society into a wilderness of solitude! I dare not keep the thought about me. Oh, here comes something to divert me.

A Countrywoman, middle-aged and poorly dressed, enters from the left.

WOMAN: (*dropping a curtsey*) I come, an't please your ladyship — you're my Lady Bountiful, an't ye?

MRS. SULLEN: Well, good woman, go on.

WOMAN: I have come seventeen long mail to have a cure for my husband's sore leg.

MRS. SULLEN: Your husband. What, woman, cure your husband!

WOMAN: Ay, poor man, for his sore leg won't let him stir from home.

MRS. SULLEN: There, I confess, you have given me a reason. Well, good woman, I'll tell you what you must do. You must lay your husband's leg upon a table, and with a chopping-knife you must lay it open as broad as you can, then you must take out the bone and beat the flesh soundly with a rolling-pin, then take salt, pepper, cloves, mace, and ginger, some sweet-herbs, and season it very well, then roll it up like brawn, and put it into the oven for two hours.

WOMAN: Heavens reward your ladyship! — I have two little babies too that are piteous bad with the graips, an't please ye.

MRS. SULLEN: (*briskly*) Put a little pepper and salt in their bellies, good woman. (*Lady Bountiful enters from the left. She wears dark satin, with an ancient cap on her head and a cape over her shoulders as if just returning from one of her many errands of mercy. Matronly and motherly, she is distinctly inclined to fleshiness. Her face is benign but not weak; her clothes suggest that there is little personal vanity in her make-up; her skirt is utilitarian, containing a large placket stuffed with medicines. Her devotion to the ailments of the poor has endowed her with something of the majesty of a queenly autocrat, beloved and adored by her subjects.*) I beg your ladyship's pardon for taking your business out of your hands; I have been a-tampering here a little with one of your patients.

LADY BOUNTIFUL: (*good-naturedly*) Come, good woman, don't mind this mad creature; I am the person that you want, I suppose. What would you have, woman?

MRS. SULLEN: She wants something for her husband's sore leg.

LADY BOUNTIFUL: What's the matter with his leg, goody?

WOMAN: It come first, as one might say, with a sort of dizziness in his foot, then he had a kind of laziness in his joints, and then his leg broke out, and then it swelled, and then it closed again, and then it broke out again, and then it festered, and then it grew better, and then it grew worse again.

MRS. SULLEN: Ha! ha! ha!

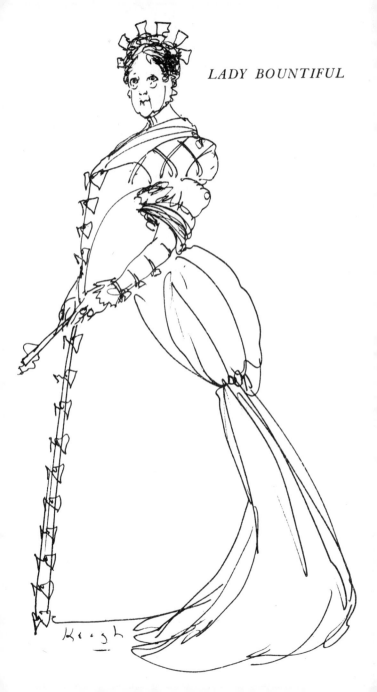

LADY BOUNTIFUL

LADY BOUNTIFUL: (*in gentle rebuke*) How can you be merry with the misfortunes of other people?

MRS. SULLEN: (*suddenly serious*) Because my own make me sad, madam.

LADY BOUNTIFUL: The worst reason in the world, daughter; your own misfortunes should teach you to pity others.

MRS. SULLEN: But the woman's misfortunes and mine are nothing alike; her husband is sick, and mine, alas! is in health.

LADY BOUNTIFUL: What! Would you have your husband sick?

MRS. SULLEN: Not of a sore leg, of all things.

LADY BOUNTIFUL: Well, good woman, go to the pantry, get your bellyful of victuals, then I'll give you a receipt of diet-drunk for your husband. But, d'ye hear, goody, you must not let your husband move too much.

WOMAN: No, no, madam, the poor man's inclinable enough to lie still.

She curtseys and goes out to the left.

LADY BOUNTIFUL: Well, daughter Sullen, though you laugh, I have done miracles about the country here with my recipts.

MRS. SULLEN: Miracles indeed if they have cured anybody; but I believe, madam, the patient's faith goes farther toward the miracle than your prescription.

LADY BOUNTIFUL: Fancy helps in some cases; but there's your husband, who has as little fancy as anybody; I brought him from death's door.

MRS. SULLEN: I suppose, madam, you made him drink plentifully of ass's milk.

Dorinda enters from the left; she runs up to Mrs. Sullen.

DORINDA: News, dear sister! news! news!

Archer runs in after her.

ARCHER: Where, where is my Lady Bountiful? — Pray, which is the old lady of you three?

LADY BOUNTIFUL: I am.

ARCHER: O madam, the fame of your ladyship's charity, goodness, benevolence, skill, and ability have drawn me hither to implore your ladyship's help in behalf of my unfortunate master, who is this moment breathing his last.

LADY BOUNTIFUL: Your master! Where is he?

ARCHER: At your gate, madam. Drawn by the appearance of your handsome house to view it nearer, and walking up the avenue within five paces of the courtyard, he was taken ill of a sudden with a sort of I know not what, but down he fell, and there he lies.

LADY BOUNTIFUL: (*calling*) Here, Scrub! Gipsy! All run, get my easy chair downstairs, put the gentleman in it, and bring him in quickly! quickly!

ARCHER: (*with great feeling*) Heaven will reward your ladyship for this charitable act.

LADY BOUNTIFUL: Is your master used to these fits?

ARCHER: O yes, madam, frequently: I have known him have five or six a night.

LADY BOUNTIFUL: What's his name?

ARCHER: (*excitedly*) Lord, madam, he's a-dying! A minute's care or neglect may save or destroy his life.

LADY BOUNTIFUL: Ah, poor gentleman! — Come, friend, show me the way; I'll see him brought in myself.

She goes off to the left with Archer.

DORINDA: O sister, my heart flutters about strangely! I can hardly forbear running to his assistance.

MRS. SULLEN: (*drily*) And I'll lay my life he deserves your assistance more than he wants it. Did not I tell you that my lord would find a way to come at you? Love's his distemper and you must be the physician; put on all your charms, summon all your fire into your eyes, plant the whole artillery of your looks against his breast, and down with him.

DORINDA: (*diffidently*) O sister! I'm but a young gunner; I shall be afraid to shoot for fear the piece should recoil and hurt myself.

MRS. SULLEN: Never fear, you shall see me shoot before you, if you will.

DORINDA: (*quickly*) No, no, dear sister; you have missed your mark so unfortunately that I shan't care for being instructed by you.

A procession enters from the left. Archer and Scrub carry a chair in which Aimwell is slumped in a counterfeit swoon. Lady Bountiful and Gipsy follow. The chair is set down in the middle of the room. Lady Bountiful is clearly in charge.

LADY BOUNTIFUL: (*extracting a small bottle from the placket in her skirt*) Here, here, let's see the hartshorn drops. — Gipsy, a glass of fair water! His fit's very strong. — Bless me, how his hands are clinched!

ARCHER: (*as Gipsy rushes off for the water*) For shame, ladies, what d'ye do? Why don't you help us? (*to Dorinda*) Pray, madam, take his hand and open it, if you can, whilst I hold his head.

DORINDA: (*kneeling beside the chair and taking his hand*) Poor gentleman! — Oh! — he has got my hand within his and squeezes it unmercifully —

LADY BOUNTIFUL: 'Tis the violence of his convulsion, child.

ARCHER: Oh, madam, he's perfectly possessed in these cases — he'll bite if you don't have a care.

DORINDA: (*screaming*) Oh, my hand! my hand!

LADY BOUNTIFUL: (*bustling up and opening Archer's grip without difficulty*) What's the matter with the foolish girl? I have got his hand open, you see, with a great deal of ease.

ARCHER: Ay, but, madam, your daughter's hand is somewhat warmer than your ladyship's, and the heat of it draws the force of the spirits that way.

MRS. SULLEN: (*in a flat, matter-of-fact tone*) I find, friend, you're very learned in these sorts of fits.

ARCHER: 'Tis no wonder, madam, for I'm often troubled with them myself. (*looking hard at Mrs. Sullen*) I find myself extremely ill at this minute.

MRS. SULLEN: (*aside*) I fancy I could find a way to cure you.

Gipsy returns with the water. Lady Bountiful drops some of her medicine in the glass and attempts, without success, to apply the glass to Aimwell's lips.

LADY BOUNTIFUL: His fit holds him very long.

ARCHER: Longer than usual, madam. — Pray, young lady, open his breast and give him air.

LADY BOUNTIFUL: (*as Dorinda opens the upper buttons of his shirt*) Where did his illness take him first, pray?

ARCHER: Today at church, madam.

LADY BOUNTIFUL: In what manner was he taken?

ARCHER: Very strangely, my lady. He was of a sudden touched with something in his eyes, which, at the first, he only felt, but could not tell whether 'twas pain or pleasure.

LADY BOUNTIFUL: Wind, nothing but wind!

ARCHER: (*looking intently at Dorinda*) By soft degrees it grew and mounted to his brain; there his fancy caught it; there formed it so beautiful and dressed it up in such gay, pleasing colors that his transported appetite seized the fair idea and straight conveyed it to his heart. That hospitable seat of life sent all its sanguine spirits forth to meet, and opened all its sluicy gates to take the stranger in.

LADY BOUNTIFUL: (*giving Gipsy the glass and reaching into her pocket for smelling salts which she waves under Aimwell's nose*) Your master should never go without a bottle to smell to. — Oh — he recovers! The lavender-water — some feathers to burn under his nose — Hungary water to rub his temples. — Oh, he comes to himself! — Hem a little, sir, hem. Gipsy! Bring the cordial-water.

Gipsy goes off with the glass. Aimwell suddenly shudders all over, then stiffens, opens his eyes, and gazes about with a glassy stare.

DORINDA: (*greatly concerned*) How d'ye, sir?

AIMWELL: (*rising as if in a hypnotic trance*) Where am I? (*gazing at Dorinda*)

> Sure I have passed the gulf of silent death,
> And now I land on the Elysian shore! —
> Behold the goddess of those happy plains,
> Fair Prosperpine[1] — let me adore thy bright divinity.

He kneels before Dorinda and kisses her hand.

MRS. SULLEN: So, so, so! I knew where the fit would end!

AIMWELL: (*still with a trance-like voice*) Eurydice[2] perhaps —

> How could thy Orpheus keep his word,
> And not look back upon thee?
> No treasure but thyself could sure have bribed him
> To look one minute off thee.

LADY BOUNTIFUL: Delirious, poor gentleman!

ARCHER: Very delirious, madam, very delirious.

AIMWELL: Martin's voice, I think.

ARCHER: Yes, my Lord. — How does your lordship?

LADY BOUNTIFUL: (*aside to Mrs. Sullen and Dorinda*) Lord! Did you mind that, girls?

AIMWELL: (*as if recovering*) Where am I?

---

[1] Queen of the underworld in classical mythology.

[2] When Eurydice died, her musician husband Orpheus descended to Hades and so charmed Pluto with his music that Orpheus was permitted to lead her back to earth on condition that he should not look back to see if she was following him. He did look back and so lost her. — Greek mythology.

ARCHER: In very good hands, sir. You were taken just now with one of your old fits, under the trees, just by this good lady's house; her ladyship had you taken in and has miraculously brought you to yourself, as you see.

AIMWELL: I am so confounded with shame, madam, that I can now only beg pardon; and refer my acknowledgments for your ladyship's care till an opportunity offers of making some amends. I dare to be no longer troublesome. — Martin! Give two guineas to the servants. (*He makes as if to leave.*)

DORINDA: (*catching him by the arm*) Sir, you may catch cold by going so soon into the air; you don't look, sir, as if you were perfectly recovered.

Aimwell pauses as if in some uncertainty and talks to Dorinda on the left side of the stage while Archer and Lady Bountiful converse at the right in dumb show.

AIMWELL: That I shall never be, madam; my present illness is so rooted that I must expect to carry it to my grave.

MRS. SULLEN: Don't despair, sir; I have known several in your distemper shake it off with a fortnight's physic.

LADY BOUNTIFUL: (*to Aimwell*) Come, sir, your servant has been telling me that you're apt to relapse if you go into the air: your good manners shan't get the better of ours — you shall sit down again, sir. (*He complies as Gipsy returns with the cordial-water.*) Come, sir, we don't mind ceremonies in the country. (*taking the glass from Gipsy and holding it out to Aimwell*) Here, sir, my service t'ye. — You shall taste my water; 'tis a cordial I can assure you, and of my own making — drink it off, sir. (*Aimwell drinks, exhibits some difficulty in getting it down gracefully, and returns the glass.*) And how d'ye find yourself now, sir?

AIMWELL: (*choking slightly*) Somewhat better — though very faint still.

LADY BOUNTIFUL: Ay, ay, people are always faint after

these fits. — Come, girls, you shall show the gentleman the house. — 'Tis but an old family building, sir; but you had better walk about and cool by degrees than venture immediately into the air. You'll find some tolerable pictures. — Dorinda, show the gentleman the way. I must go to the poor woman below.

She exits to the left. Aimwell rises.

DORINDA: This way, sir. (*indicated an exit at the right*)

AIMWELL: Ladies, shall I beg leave for my servant to wait on you, for he understands pictures very well?

MRS. SULLEN: Sir, we understand originals as well as he does pictures, so he may come along.

Exeunt all but Scrub, Aimwell accompanying Dorinda. As soon as they have left the stage, Foigard enters from the left.

FOIGARD: Save you, Master Scrub!

SCRUB: Sir, I won't be saved your way — I hate a priest, I abhor the French, and I defy the devil. Sir, I'm a bold Briton and will spill the last drop of my blood to keep out popery and slavery.

FOIGARD: Master Scrub, you would put me down in politics, and so I would be speaking with Mrs. Shipsy.

SCRUB: Good Mr. Priest, you can't speak with her; she's sick, sir, she's gone abroad, sir she's — dead two months ago, sir.

Gipsy re-enters from the right.

GIPSY: How now, impudence! How dare you talk so saucily to the doctor? — Pray, sir, don't take it ill; for the common people of England are not so civil to strangers, as —

SCRUB: You lie! You lie! 'Tis the common people that are civilest to strangers.

GIPSY: Sirrah, I have a good mind to — get you out, I say!

SCRUB: I won't.

GIPSY: You won't, sauce-box! — Pray, doctor, what is

the captain's name that came to your inn last night?

SCRUB: *(aside)* The captain! Ah, the devil, there she hampers me again; the captain has me on one side and the priest on t'other: so between the gown and the sword, I have a fine time on't. — But *Cedunt arma togae.*[3]

He starts off to the right.

GIPSY: What, sirrah, won't you march?

SCRUB: No, my dear, I won't march — but I'll walk. *(aside)* And I'll make bold to listen a little too. *(He goes behind the side-scene and listens.)*

GIPSY: *(confidentially)* Indeed, doctor, the Count has been barbarously treated; that's the truth on't.

FOIGARD: Ah, Mrs. Gipsy, upon my shoul, now, gra, his complainings would mollify the marrow in your bones and move the bowels of your commiseration! He veeps, and he dances, and he fistles, and he swears, and he laughs, and he stamps, and he sings; in conclusion, joy, he's afflicted *à-la-Française* and a stranger would not know whider to cry or to laugh with him.

GIPSY: What would you have me do, doctor?

FOIGARD: Nothing, joy, but only hide the Count in Mrs. Sullen's closet when it is dark.

GIPSY: *(seemingly horrified)* Nothing! Is that nothing? It would be both a sin and a shame, doctor.

FOIGARD: *(offering her a purse)* Here is twenty louis-d'ors, for your shame, and I will give you an absolution for the shin.

GIPSY: *(weakening)* But won't that money look like a bribe?

FOIGARD: Dat is according as you shall tauk it. If you receive the money beforehand, 'twill be *logicè*,[4] a bribe; but if you stay till afterwards, 'twill be only a gratification.

---

[3] "The soldier defers to the priest."

[4] According to logic.

GIPSY: (*taking the money*) Well, doctor, I'll take it *logicè*. But what must I do with my conscience, sir?

FOIGARD: Leave dat wid me, joy; I am your priest, gra; and your conscience is under my hands.

GIPSY: (*still somewhat hesitant*) But should I put the Count into the closet —

FOIGARD: Vel, is dere any shin for a man's being in a closhet? One may go to prayers in a closhet.

GIPSY: But if the lady should come into her chamber and go to bed?

FOIGARD: Vel, and is dere any shin in going to bed, joy?

GIPSY: Ay, but if the parties should meet, doctor?

FOIGARD: Vel den — the parties must be responsible. Do you be gone after putting the Count into the closhet; and leave the shins wid themselves. I will come with the Count to instruct you in your chamber.

GIPSY: Well, doctor, your religion is so pure! Methinks I'm so easy after an absolution and can sin afresh with so much security that I'm resolved to die a martyr to't. Here's the key of the garden door. Come in the back way when 'tis late — I'll be ready to receive you; but don't so much as whisper, only take hold of my hand; I'll lead you, and do you lead the Count and follow me.

She takes his hand as if by way of demonstration and leads him off to the left.

SCRUB: (*emerging from hiding*) What witchcraft now have these two imps of the devil been a-hatching here? "There's twenty louis-d'ors"; I heard that and saw the purse. — (*indicating his awareness that the others are about to return, and going off to the left*) But I must give room to my betters.

He disappears, left, just as Aimwell, leading Dorinda and making love in dumb show re-enters form the right, followed by Mrs. Sullen and Archer.

MRS. SULLEN: (*to Archer*) Pray, sir, how d'ye like that piece? (*indicating the painting of Jupiter and the Swan*)

ARCHER: Oh, 'tis Leda! You find, madam, how Jupiter comes disguised to make love —

MRS. SULLEN: (*rapidly changing the subject*) But what think you there of Alexander's battles?

ARCHER: We only want a Le Brun, madam, to draw greater battles, and a greater general of our own. The Danube, madam, would make a greater figure in a picture than the Granicus; and we have our Ramillies to match their Arbela.[5]

MRS. SULLEN: Pray, sir, what head is that in the corner there?

ARCHER: O madam, 'tis poor Ovid in his exile.

MRS. SULLEN: What was he banished for?

ARCHER: His ambitious love, madam. (*bowing*) His misfortune touches me.

MRS. SULLEN: (*off-handedly*) Was he successful in his amours?

ARCHER: There he has left us in the dark. (*meaningfully*) He was too much a gentleman to tell.

MRS. SULLEN: If he were secret, I pity him.

ARCHER: (*looking at her*) And if he were successful, I envy him.

MRS. SULLEN: (*again changing the subject*) How d'ye like that Venus over the chimney?

ARCHER: Venus! I protest, madam, I took it for your picture; but now I look again, 'tis not handsome enough.

MRS. SULLEN: Oh, what a charm is flattery! If you would see my picture, there it is over that cabinet. How d'ye like it?

---

[5] These paintings are described on p. 111. The battle of the river Granicus resulted in the first defeat of Darius by Alexander. At the Battle of Ramillies Marlborough defeated the French just as Alexander routed Darius at the Battle of Arbela.

ARCHER: I must admire anything, madam, that has the least resemblance of you. But methinks, madam — (*He looks at the picture and Mrs. Sullen three or four times, by turns*) Pray, madam, who drew it?

MRS. SULLEN: A famous hand, sir.

Aimwell and Dorinda, still wrapped up in each other, go off to the left.

ARCHER: A famous hand, madam! — Your eyes, indeed, are featured there; but where's the sparkling moisture, shining fluid, in which they swim? The picture, indeed, has your dimples; but where's the swarm of killing Cupids that should ambush there? The lips too are figured out; but where's the carnation dew, the pouting ripeness that tempts the taste in the original?

MRS. SULLEN: (*aside*) Had it been my lot to have matched with such a man!

ARCHER: Your breasts too — presumptuous man! What, paint Heaven! Apropos, madam, in the very next picture is Salmoneus that was struck dead with lightning for offering to imitate Jove's thunder; I hope you served the painter so, madam?

MRS. SULLEN: Had my eyes the power of thunder, they should employ their lightning better.

ARCHER: (*looking off to the right*) There's the finest bed in that room, madam! I suppose 'tis your ladyship's bedchamber.

MRS. SULLEN: And what then, sir?

ARCHER: I think the quilt is the richest that ever I saw. I can't at this distance, madam, distinguish the figures of the embroidery; will you give me leave, madam?

MRS. SULLEN: (*aside*) The devil take his impudence! — Sure, if I gave him an opportunity, he durst not offer it? — I have a great mind to try. — (*She moves to the right as if to oblige Archer but hesitates at the edge of the stage.*) 'Sdeath, what am I doing? — And alone, too! (*running off to the right*) Sister! Sister!

ARCHER: (*starting to follow her off in a leisurely and self-assured manner*) I'll follow her close —

> For where a Frenchman durst attempt to storm,
> A Briton sure may well the work perform.

His exit is interrupted by the sudden appearance of Scrub who meets him head-on.

SCRUB: Martin! Brother Martin!

ARCHER: O brother Scrub, I beg your pardon; I was not a-going: here's a guinea my master ordered you.

SCRUB: (*snatching the coin*) A guinea! Hi! hi! hi! a guinea! eh — by this light it is a guinea! But I suppose you expect one-and-twenty shillings in change?

ARCHER: Not at all; I have another for Gipsy.

SCRUB: A guinea for her! Faggot and fire for the witch! Sir, give me that guinea, and I'll discover a plot.

ARCHER: A plot!

SCRUB: Ay, sir, a plot, and a horrid plot! First, it must be a plot because there's a woman in't; secondly, it must be a plot because there's a priest in't; thirdly, it must be a plot because there's French gold in't; and fourthly, it must be a plot because I don't know what to make on't.

ARCHER: Nor anybody else, I'm afraid, brother Scrub.

SCRUB: (*confidentially*) Truly, I'm afraid so, too; for where there's a priest and a woman, there's always a mystery and a riddle. This I know, that here has been the doctor with a temptation in one hand and an absolution in the other, and Gipsy has sold herself to the devil. I saw the price paid down; my eyes shall take their oath on't.

ARCHER: And is all this bustle about Gipsy?

SCRUB: That's not all. I could hear but a word here and there; but I remember they mentioned a Count, a closet, a back-door, and a key.

ARCHER: (*slightly startled out of his amused attitude*) The Count! — Did you hear nothing of Mrs. Sullen?

SCRUB: I did hear some word that sounded that way; but whether it was Sullen or Dorinda I could not distinguish.

ARCHER: You have told this matter to nobody, brother?

SCRUB: Told! No, sir, I thank you for that. I'm resolved never to speak one word *pro* nor *con* till we have a peace.

ARCHER: You're i' the right, brother Scrub. Here's a treaty afoot between the Count and the lady: the priest and the chambermaid are the plenipotentiaries. It shall go hard but I find a way to be included in the treaty. — Where's the doctor now?

SCRUB: He and Gipsy are this moment devouring my lady's marmalade in the closet.

AIMWELL: (*calling from the left*) Martin! Martin!

ARCHER: I come, sir, I come.

SCRUB: But you forget the other guinea, brother Martin.

ARCHER: Here, I give it with all my heart.

SCRUB: And I take it with all my soul. (*Archer exits to the left.*) Ecod, I'll spoil your plotting, Mrs. Gipsy! and if you should set the captain upon me, these two guineas will buy me off.

He follows Archer off. After a moment, Mrs. Sullen re-enters from the right and meets Dorinda who comes on from the left.

MRS. SULLEN: Well, sister!

DORINDA: And well, sister!

MRS. SULLEN: What's become of my lord?

DORINDA: What's become of his servant?

MRS. SULLEN: Servant! He's a prettier fellow and a finer gentleman by fifty degrees than his master.

DORINDA: O' my conscience, I fancy you could beg that fellow at the gallows-foot!

MRS. SULLEN: O' my conscience I could, provided I could put a friend of yours in his room.

DORINDA: *(sternly)* You desired me, sister, to leave you when you transgressed the bounds of honor.

MRS. SULLEN: Thou dear censorious country girl! what dost mean? You can't think of the man without the bedfellow, I find.

DORINDA: *(with quaint simplicity)* I don't find anything unnatural in that thought: while the mind is conversant with flesh and blood, it must conform to the humors of the company.

MRS. SULLEN: *(brightening)* How a little love and good company improves a woman! Why, child, you begin to live — you never spoke before.

DORINDA: Because I was never spoke to. — My lord has told me that I have more wit and beauty than any of my sex; and truly I begin to think the man is sincere.

MRS. SULLEN: You're in the right, Dorinda; pride is the life of a woman, and flattery is our daily bread; and she's a fool that won't believe a man there, as much as she that believes him in anything else. But I'll lay you a guinea that I had finer things said to me than you had.

DORINDA: Done! What did your fellow say to ye?

MRS. SULLEN: My fellow took the picture of Venus for mine.

DORINDA: But my lover took me for Venus herself.

MRS. SULLEN: *(scornfully)* Common cant! Had my spark called me a Venus directly, I should have believed him a footman in good earnest.

DORINDA: But my lover was upon his knees to me.

MRS. SULLEN: And mine was upon his tiptoes to me.

DORINDA: Mine swore to die for me.

MRS. SULLEN: Mine swore to die with me.

DORINDA: Mine spoke the softest moving things.

MRS. SULLEN: Mine had his moving things too.

DORINDA: Mine kissed my hand ten thousand times.

MRS. SULLEN: Mine has all that pleasure to come.

DORINDA: *(triumphantly)* Mine offered marriage.

MRS. SULLEN: (*cynically*) O Lard! D'ye call that a moving thing?

DORINDA: The sharpest arrow in his quiver, my dear sister! Why, my ten thousand pounds may lie brooding here this seven years and hatch nothing at last but some ill-natured clown like yours. Whereas if I marry my Lord Aimwell, there will be title, place, and precedence, the Park, the play, and the drawing-room, splendor, equipage, noise, and flambeaux. — *Hey, my Lady Aimwell's servants there! — Lights, lights to the stairs! — My Lady Aimwell's coach put forward! — Stand by, make room for her ladyship!* — Are not these things moving? — What! melancholy of a sudden?

MRS. SULLEN: (*sombrely*) Happy, happy sister! Your angel has been watchful for your happiness whilst mine has slept regardless of his charge. Long smiling years of circling joys for you, but not one hour for me! (*She weeps.*)

DORINDA: (*putting her arm around her*) Come, my dear, we'll talk of something else.

MRS. SULLEN: O Dorinda! I own myself a woman, full of my sex, a gentle, generous soul, easy and yielding to soft desires; a spacious heart where love and all his train might lodge. And must the fair apartment of my breast be made a stable for a brute to lie in?

DORINDA: (*gently*) Meaning your husband, I suppose?

MRS. SULLEN: Husband! No; even husband is too soft a name for him. — But come, I expect my brother here tonight or tomorrow; he was abroad when my father married me; perhaps he'll find a way to make me easy.

DORINDA: Will you promise not to make yourself easy in the meantime with my lord's friend?

MRS. SULLEN: (*stepping away and taking Dorinda's hands in hers*) You mistake me, sister. It happens with us as among the men: the greatest talkers are the greatest cowards. And there's a reason for it: those spirits evaporate in prattle which might do more mischief if they took another course. — Though, to confess the truth, I do love that fellow — and if I met him dressed as he should be, and I undressed as I should be — look'ee, sister, I have no supernatural gifts — I can't swear I could resist the temptation; though I can safely promise to avoid it; and that's as much as the best of us can do.

She gives Dorinda a slight hug; then, arms around each other's waists, they go off to the right.

SCENE TWO

Back at Boniface's inn, shortly after. Aimwell and Archer enter from the right, returning from Lady Bountiful's. They are in high spirits.

ARCHER: *(laughing)* And the awkward kindness of the good motherly old gentlewoman —

AIMWELL: And the coming easiness of the young one — 'Sdeath, 'tis pity to deceive her!

ARCHER: Nay, if you adhere to these principles, stop where you are.

AIMWELL: *(becoming serious)* I can't stop, for I love her to distraction.

ARCHER: 'Sdeath, if you love her a hair's-breadth beyond discretion, you must go no further.

AIMWELL: Well, well, anything to deliver us from sauntering away our idle evenings at White's, Tom's,[6] or Will's, and be stinted to bear looking at our old acquaintance, the cards; because our impotent pockets can't afford us a guinea for the mercenary drabs.

ARCHER: Or be obliged to some purse-proud coxcomb for a scandalous bottle, where we must not pretend to our share of the discourse because we can't pay our club[7] o' th' reckoning. — Damn it, I had rather sponge

---

[6] A coffee house on the same street as Will's; it became very popular as a fashionable resort after the performance of this play.
[7] Share of the total bill.

upon Morris and sup upon a dish of bohea[8] scored behind the door!

AIMWELL: And there expose our want of sense by talking criticisms, as we should our want of money by railing at the government.

ARCHER: Or be obliged to sneak into the side-box, and between both houses steal two acts of a play, and because we han't money to see the other three, we come away discontented, and damn the whole five.[9]

AIMWELL: And ten thousand such rascally tricks — had we outlived our fortunes among our acquaintance. — But now —

ARCHER: Ay, now is the time to prevent all this: — strike while the iron is hot. — This priest is the luckiest part of our adventure; he shall marry you and pimp for me.

AIMWELL: But I should not like a woman that can be so fond of a Frenchman.

ARCHER: Alas, sir! Necessity has no law. The lady may be in distress; perhaps she has a confounded husband, and her revenge may carry her farther than her love. Egad, I have so good an opinion of her, and of myself, that I begin to fancy strange things: and we must say this for the honor of our women, and indeed of ourselves, that they do stick to their men as they do to their *Magna Charta*. If the plot lies as I suspect, I must put on the gentleman. — But here comes the doctor — I shall be ready.

He goes off, left, to his room. Foigard enters from the right.

FOIGARD: Sauve you, noble friend.

AIMWELL: O sir, your servant! Pray, doctor, may I crave your name?

---

[8] Black tea, served at Morris' Coffee House.
[9] Alluding to the custom that anyone who left the theatre before the conclusion of the act of the play which was in progress when he entered should not be charged admission.

FOIGARD: Fat naam is upon me? Me naam is Foigard, joy.

AIMWELL: Foigard! a very good name for a clergyman. Pray, Doctor Foigard, were you ever in Ireland?

FOIGARD: Ireland! No, joy. Fat sort of plaace is dat saam Ireland? Dey say de people are catched dere when dey are young.

AIMWELL: And some of 'em when they are old: — as for example — (*taking Foigard by the shoulder*) Sir, I arrest you as a traitor against the government; you're a subject of England, and this morning showed me a commission by which you served as chaplain in the French army. This is death by our law, and your reverence must hang for it.

FOIGARD: (*trembling and blustering simultaneously*) Upon my shoul, noble friend, dis is strange news you tell me! Fader Foigard a subject of England! de son of a burgomaster of Brussels, a subject of England! ubooboo — [10]

AIMWELL: (*severely*) The son of a bog-trotter in Ireland! Sir, your tongue will condemn you before any bench in the kingdom.

FOIGARD: (*brightening*) And is my tongue all your evidensh, joy?

AIMWELL: That's enough.

FOIGARD: No, no, joy, for I vill never spake English no more.

AIMWELL: Sir, I have other evidence. — Here, Martin! (*Archer re-enters.*) You know this fellow?

ARCHER: (*in a brogue*) Saave you, my dear cussen, how does your health?

FOIGARD: (*aside*) Ah! upon my shoul dere is my countryman, and his brogue will hang mine. (*to Archer*) *Mynheer, Ick wet neat watt hey zacht; Ick universton ewe neat, sacramant!* [11]

---

[10] An Irish dialectical exclamation.

[11] A garbled pseudo-German, meaning "Sir, I do not know what you say; I don't understand you."

AIMWELL: Altering your language won't do, sir; this fellow knows your person and will swear to your face.

FOIGARD: Faash! fey, is dere a brogue upon my faash too?

ARCHER: Upon my soulvation dere ish, joy! — But cussen Macksane, vil you not put a remembrance upon me?

FOIGARD: (*aside*) Mackshane! By St. Patrick, dat ish my naam shure enough!

AIMWELL: (*aside to Archer*) I fancy, Archer, you have it.

FOIGARD: The devil hang you, joy? By fat acquaintance are you my cussen?

ARCHER: (*enthusiastically*) Oh, de devil hang yourshelf, joy! you know we were little boys togeder upon de school, and your foster-moder's son was married upon my nurse's chister, joy, and so we are Irish cussens.

FOIGARD: De devil taake de relation! Vel, joy, and fat school was it?

ARCHER: I tinks it vas — aay — 'twas Tipperary.[12]

FOIGARD: No, no, joy; it vas Kilkenny.

AIMWELL: That's enough for us — self-confession. — Come, sir, we must deliver you into the hands of the next magistrate.

ARCHER: He sends you to jail, you're tried next assizes, and away you go swing into purgatory.

FOIGARD: (*pitiably, to Archer*) And is it so wid you, cussen?

ARCHER: (*with brisk efficiency*) It vil be sho wid you, cussen, if you don't immediately confess the secret between you and Mrs. Gipsy. Look'ee, sir, the gallows or the secret, take your choice.

FOIGARD: The gallows! Upon my shoul I hate that

---

[12] A free grammar school founded in 1669. Kilkenny, mentioned in the next line, was founded in 1684. Swift, Congreve, and Berkeley were educated there.

saam gallow, for it is a diseash dat is fatal to our family. Vel, den, dere is nothing, shentlemens, but Mrs. Shullen would spaak wid the Count in her chamber at midnight, and dere is not haarm, joy, for I am to conduct the Count to the plash, myshelf.

ARCHER: As I guessed. Have you communicated the matter to the Count?

FOIGARD: I have not sheen him since.

ARCHER: Right again! Why then, doctor — you shall conduct me to the lady instead of the Count.

FOIGARD: Fat, my cussen to the lady! Upon my shoul, gra, dat is too much upon the brogue.

ARCHER: (*with light confidence*) Come, come, doctor; consider we have got a rope about your neck, and if you offer to squeak, we'll stop your windpipe most certainly: we shall have another job for you in a day or two, I hope.

AIMWELL: (*looking off to the right*) Here's company coming this way; let's into my chamber, and there concert our affairs farther.

ARCHER: (*following Aimwell off to the left and holding Foigard by the arm*) Come, my dear cussen, come along.

When they have left the stage, Boniface, Hounslow, and Bagshot enter together from a proscenium door at the right; Gibbet enters from the opposite door.

GIBBET: (*conspiratorially*) Well, gentlemen, 'tis a fine night for our enterprise.

HOUNSLOW: Dark as hell.

BAGSHOT: And blows like the devil; our landlord here has showed us the window where we must break in, and tells us the plate stands in the wainscot cupboard in the parlor.

BONIFACE: Ay, ay, Mr. Bagshot, as the saying is, knives and forks, and cups and cans, and tumblers and tankards. There's one tankard, as the saying is, that's near upon as big as me; it was a present to the squire from his godmother and smells of nutmeg and toast like an East-India ship.

HOUNSLOW: Then you say we must divide at the stairhead?

BONIFACE: Yes, Mr. Hounslow, as the saying is. At one end of that gallery lies my Lady Bountiful and her daughter, and at the other Mrs. Sullen. As for the squire —

GIBBET: He's safe enough. I have fairly entered him, and he's more than half seas over already. But such a parcel of scoundrels are got about him now that, egad, I was ashamed to be seen in their company.

BONIFACE: 'Tis now twelve, as the saying is — gentlemen, you must set out at one.

GIBBET: Hounslow, do you and Bagshot see our arms fixed, and I'll come to you presently.

HOUNSLOW, BAGSHOT: We will.

Hounslow and Bagshot go off to the left.

GIBBET: Well, my dear Bonny, you assure me that Scrub is a coward?

BONIFACE: A chicken, as the saying is. You'll have no creature to deal with but the ladies.

GIBBET: And I can assure you, friend, there's a great deal of address and good manners in robbing a lady; I am the most a gentleman that way that ever travelled the road. — But, my dear Bonny, this prize will be a galleon, a Vigo[13] business. I warrant you we shall bring off three or four thousand pounds.

BONIFACE: In plate, jewels, and money, as the saying is, you may.

GIBBET: Why, then Tyburn,[14] I defy thee! I'll get up to the town, sell off my horse and arms, buy myself some pretty employment in the household, and be as snug and as honest as any courtier of 'em all.

---

[13] A brilliant British naval victory.
[14] The usual place of execution in Middlesex.

BONIFACE: And what think you then of my daughter Cherry for a wife?

GIBBET: Look'ee, my dear Bonny — Cherry *is the Goddess I adore,* as the song goes; but it is a maxim that man and wife should never have it in their power to hang one another; for if they should, the Lord have mercy on 'em both!

They go off to the left.

MRS. SULLEN

Act Five

The scene is the same. It is about two A.M. at Boni-
face's Inn. There is a vociferous knocking at the outside
proscenium door. Boniface comes running in from the
left.

BONIFACE: Coming! Coming! — A coach and six
foaming horses at this time o'night! Some great man,
as the saying is, for he scorns to travel with other people.

He opens the door to admit Sir Charles Freeman,
Mrs. Sullen's older brother. He is quite sedately dressed,
in black velvet cape, black frock coat, white trousers,
and boots.

SIR CHARLES: What, fellow! A public house, and abed
when other people sleep?

BONIFACE: Sir, I an't abed, as the saying is.

SIR CHARLES: Is Mr. Sullen's family abed, think'ee?

BONIFACE: All but the squire himself, sir, as the saying is; he's in the house.

SIR CHARLES: What company has he?

BONIFACE: Why, sir, there's the constable, Mr. Gage
the exciseman, the hunch-backed barber, and two or
three other gentlemen.

SIR CHARLES: (*aside*) I find my sister's letters gave me
the true picture of her spouse.

Squire Sullen, drunk, comes staggering in from the
left.

BONIFACE: Sir, here's the squire.

SQUIRE SULLEN: (*mumbling*) The puppies left me
asleep — Sir!

SIR CHARLES: (*coldly*) Well, sir.

SQUIRE SULLEN: (*with maudlin vehemence*) Sir, I am an unfortunate man — I have three thousand pounds a year, and I can't get a man to drink a cup of ale with me.

SIR CHARLES: That's very hard.

SQUIRE SULLEN: Ay, sir; and unless you have pity upon me and smoke one pipe with me, I must e'en go home to my wife, and I had rather go to the devil by half.

SIR CHARLES: But I presume, sir, you won't see your wife tonight; she'll be gone to bed. You don't use to lie with your wife in that pickle?

SQUIRE SULLEN: What! not lie with my wife! Why, sir, do you take me for an atheist or a rake?

SIR CHARLES: If you hate her, sir, I think you had better lie from her.

SQUIRE SULLEN: (*ponderously*) I think so too, friend. But I'm Justice of Peace, and must do nothing against the law.

SIR CHARLES: (*with increasing hostility*) Law! As I take it, Mr. Justice, nobody observes law for law's sake, only for the good of those for whom it was made.

SQUIRE SULLEN: (*shrugging his shoulders*) But if the law orders me to send you to jail, you must lie there, my friend.

SIR CHARLES: Not unless I commit a crime to deserve it.

SQUIRE SULLEN: (*with a drunken guffaw*) A crime? 'Onns, ain't I married?

SIR CHARLES: (*subduing his antagonism as if deciding to attempt to cope with his brother-in-law*) Nay, sir, if you call marriage a crime, you must disown it for a law.

SQUIRE SULLEN: Eh! I must be acquainted with you, sir. — But, sir, I should be very glad to know the truth of this matter.

SIR CHARLES: Truth, sir, is a profound sea, and few there be that dare wade deep enough to find out the bottom on't. Besides, sir, I'm afraid the line of your understanding mayn't be long enough.

SQUIRE SULLEN: Look'ee, sir, I have nothing to say to your sea of truth, but if a good parcel of land can entitle a man to a little truth, I have as much as any he in the country.

BONIFACE: I never heard your worship, as the saying is, talk so much before.

SQUIRE SULLEN: Because I never met with a man that I liked before.

BONIFACE: Pray, sir, as the saying is, let me ask you one question: are not man and wife one flesh?

SIR CHARLES: You and your wife, Mr. Guts, may be one flesh because ye are nothing else; but rational creatures have minds that must be united.

SQUIRE SULLEN: Minds!

SIR CHARLES: Ay, minds, sir; don't you think that the mind takes place of the body?

SQUIRE SULLEN: In some people.

SIR CHARLES: Then the interest of the master must be consulted before that of his servant.

SQUIRE SULLEN: (*clapping Sir Charles affectionately on the back*) Sir, you shall dine with me tomorrow! — 'Oons, I always thought that we were naturally one.

SIR CHARLES: Sir, I know that my two hands are naturally one because they love one another, kiss one another, help one another in all the actions of life; but I could not say so much if they were always at cuffs.

SQUIRE SULLEN: (*with exaggerated concentration*)Then 'tis plain that we are two.

SIR CHARLES: Why don't you part with her, sir?

SQUIRE SULLEN: (*his face lighting up*) Will you take her, sir?

SIR CHARLES: With all my heart.

SQUIRE SULLEN: You shall have her tomorrow morning, and a venison-pastry into the bargain.

SIR CHARLES: You'll let me have her fortune too?

SQUIRE SULLEN: (*broadly*) Fortune! Why, sir, I have no quarrel at her fortune: I only hate the woman, sir, and none but the woman shall go.

SIR CHARLES: But her fortune, sir —

SQUIRE SULLEN: Can you play at whisk,[1] sir?

SIR CHARLES: No, truly, sir.

SQUIRE SULLEN: Nor at all-fours? [2]

SIR CHARLES: Neither.

SQUIRE SULLEN: (*aside*) 'Oons! Where was this man bred? (*aloud*) Burn me, sir! I can't go home, 'tis but two a clock.

SIR CHARLES: For half an hour, sir, if you please; but you must consider 'tis late.

SQUIRE SULLEN: Late! That's the reason I can't go to bed. Come, sir!

They go off together to the left. Suddenly, Cherry runs in from the right, crosses the stage, and knocks at Aimwell's chamber door. Aimwell opens the door and comes out in his nightcap and gown.

AIMWELL: What's the matter? You tremble, child; you're frightened.

CHERRY: (*breathlessly*) No wonder, sir — But, in short, sir, this very minute a gang of rogues are gone to rob my Lady Bountiful's house.

AIMWELL: (*in complete surprise*) How!

CHERRY: I dogged 'em to the very door and left 'em breaking in.

AIMWELL: Have you alarmed anybody else with the news?

CHERRY: No, no, sir, I wanted to have discovered the whole plot, and twenty other things, to your man

---

[1] Whist.

[2] High, low, Jack, and the game.

Martin; but I have searched the whole house, and can't find him: where is he?

AIMWELL: No matter, child; will you guide me immediately to the house?

CHERRY: With all my heart, sir; my Lady Bountiful is my godmother, and I love Mistress Dorinda so well —

AIMWELL: Dorinda! the name inspires me, the glory and the danger shall be my own. — Come, my life, let me but get my sword.

He darts back into his room, rushes out immediately with his sword in his right hand, seizes Cherry's hand with his left and dashes with her to the outside door, right.

SCENE TWO

Mrs. Sullen's bedchamber, shortly afterward. In the center is an ornate bed with crowned canopy and curtains at the head attached to the rear panelled wall. Mrs. Sullen and Dorinda, in nightshifts, are discovered sitting on either side of a table at the left of the bed, Mrs. Sullen next to the bed and Dorinda opposite. Lighted candles are on the table and in wall-sconces.

DORINDA: 'Tis very late, sister, no news of your spouse yet?

MRS. SULLEN: (*wearily*) No, I'm condemned to be alone till towards four, and then perhaps I may be executed with his company.

DORINDA: Well, my dear, I'll leave you to your rest; you'll go directly to bed, I suppose?

MRS. SULLEN: I don't know what to do. — Heigh-ho!

DORINDA: That's a desiring sigh, sister.

MRS. SULLEN: This is a languishing hour, sister.

DORINDA: And might prove a critical minute if the pretty fellow were here.

MRS. SULLEN: (*brightening*) Here! What, in my bedchamber at two o'clock o' th' morning, I undressed, the family asleep, my hated husband abroad, and my lovely fellow at my feet! — O'gad, sister!

DORINDA: (*with an indulgent smile*) Thoughts are free, sister, and them I allow you. — So, my dear, good night.

MRS. SULLEN: A good rest to my dear Dorinda! (*Dorinda kisses her and retires to the left.*) Thoughts free! Are they so? Why, then, suppose him here, dressed like a youthful, gay, and burning bridegroom, (*A proscenium door at the right, behind Mrs. Sullen's back, opens quietly. Archer steals out of the closet and to the foot of the bed.*) with tongue enchanting, eyes bewitching, knees imploring. (*Suiting her words, Archer kneels and holds out his hands toward her. Hearing a rustle, she turns a little on one side and sees him.*) Ah! (*She shrieks, jumps up, and runs to the other side of the table.*) Have my thoughts raised a spirit? — What are you, sir, a man or a devil?

ARCHER: (*rising*) A man, a man, madam.

MRS. SULLEN: (*still trembling*) How shall I be sure of it?

ARCHER: (*approaching her*) Madam, I'll give you demonstration this minute. (*He takes her hand.*)

MRS. SULLEN: (*at once frightened and enchanted*) What, sir! Do you intend to be rude?

ARCHER: Yes, madam, if you please.

MRS. SULLEN: (*now quite recovered*) In the name of wonder, whence came ye?

ARCHER: From the skies, madam — I'm Jupiter in love, and you shall be my Alcmena.[3]

MRS. SULLEN: How came you in?

ARCHER: I flew in at the window, madam; your cousin Cupid lent me his wings and your sister Venus opened the casement.

MRS. SULLEN: I'm struck dumb with wonder!

---

[3] Jupiter enjoyed Alcmena's love by assuming the shape of her husband.

ARCHER: (*looking passionately at her*) And I — with admiration!

MRS. SULLEN: (*as if saying the expected thing*) What will become of me?

ARCHER: (*stepping back as if to admire a masterpiece of art*) How beautiful she looks! The teeming, jolly spring smiles in her blooming face, and, when she was conceived, her mother smelt to roses, looked on lilies —

> Lilies unfold their white, their fragrant charms,
> When the warm sun thus darts into their arms.

He dashes forward as he speaks and embraces her.
MRS. SULLEN: (*with a shriek*) Ah!

ARCHER: (*sternly as he partially releases her*) 'Oons, madam, what d'ye mean? You'll raise the house.

MRS. SULLEN: (*angrily*) Sir, I'll wake the dead before I bear this! — What! approach me with the freedom of a keeper! I'm glad on't, your impudence has cured me.

ARCHER: (*stepping back and kneeling*) If this be impudence — I leave to your partial self; no panting pilgrim, after a tedious, painful voyage, e'er bowed before his saint with more devotion.

MRS. SULLEN: (*aside*) Now, now, I'm ruined if he kneels! (*aloud*) Rise, thou prostrate engineer, not all thy undermining skill shall reach my heart. Rise, and know I am a woman without my sex; I can love to all the tenderness of wishes, sighs, and tears — (*quickly as he rises and approaches her*) But go no farther. — Still, to convince you that I'm more than woman, I can speak my frailty, confess my weakness even for you, but —

ARCHER: (*ardently holding out his arms*) For me!

MRS. SULLEN: (*evading him*) Hold, sir! Build not upon that; for my most mortal hatred follows if you disobey what I command you now. — Leave me this minute. (*aside*) If he denies, I'm lost.

ARCHER: Then you'll promise —

MRS. SULLEN: Anything another time.

ARCHER: When shall I come?

MRS. SULLEN: (*weakly*) Tomorrow — when you will.

ARCHER: Your lips must seal the promise.

MRS. SULLEN: (*unconvincingly*) Psha!

ARCHER: They must! they must! (*kissing her*) Raptures and paradise! — And why not now, my angel? The time, the place, silence, and secrecy all conspire. (*taking her in his arms*) And the now conscious stars have preordained this moment for my happiness.

MRS. SULLEN: (*faintly*) You will not! cannot, sure!

ARCHER: If the sun rides fast and disappoints not mortals of tomorrow's dawn, this night shall crown my joys.

MRS. SULLEN: My sex's pride assist me!

ARCHER: My sex's strength help me!

MRS. SULLEN: (*struggling*) You shall kill me first!

ARCHER: (*picking her up in his arms*) I'll die with you.

MRS. SULLEN: Thieves! thieves! murder!

Scrub comes running in from the left in shirt-sleeves and wearing only one shoe.

SCRUB: Thieves! thieves! murder! popery!

ARCHER: (*dropping Mrs. Sullen on the bed, wheeling around, and drawing his sword*) Ha! The very timorous stag will kill in rutting time.

SCRUB: (*dropping to his knees*) O pray, sir, spare all I have and take my life!

MRS. SULLEN: (*seizing hold of Archer's sword-hand from behind*) What does the fellow mean?

SCRUB: O madam, down upon your knees, your marrow-bones! He's one of 'em.

ARCHER: Of whom?

SCRUB: One of the rogues — I beg your pardon, one of the honest gentlemen that just now are broke into the house.

ARCHER: How!

MRS. SULLEN: I hope you did not come to rob me?

ARCHER: (*turning to her*) Indeed I did, madam, but

I would have taken nothing but what you might ha'
spared; but your crying "Thieves" has waked this
dreaming fool, and so he takes 'em for granted.

SCRUB: (*trembling*) Granted! 'Tis granted, sir; take all
we have.

MRS. SULLEN: The fellow looks as if he were broke out
of bedlam.[4]

SCRUB: 'Oons, madam, they've broke into the house
with fire and sword! I saw them, heard them; they'll be
here this minute.

ARCHER: What, thieves!

SCRUB: Under favor, sir, I think so.

MRS. SULLEN: (*tremulously*) What shall we do, sir?

ARCHER: (*kissing her hand and dropping it*) Madam,
I wish your ladyship a good night.

MRS. SULLEN: (*reaching out to him*) Will you leave me?

ARCHER: Leave you! Lord, madam, did you not command me to be gone just now, upon pain of your im-
mortal hatred?

MRS. SULLEN: (*clutching at him*) Nay, but, pray, sir —

ARCHER: Ha! ha! ha! Now comes my turn to be
ravished. — You see now, madam, you must use men
one way or other; but take this by the way, good
madam, that none but a fool will give you the benefit
of his courage unless you'll take his love along with it.
(*to Scrub*) How are they armed, friend?

SCRUB: With sword and pistol, sir.

ARCHER: Hush! — I see a dark lantern coming through
the gallery. Madam, be assured I will protect you, or
lose my life.

MRS. SULLEN: Your life! No, sir, they can rob me of
nothing that I value half so much; therefore now, sir,
let me entreat you to be gone.

ARCHER: No, madam, I'll consult my own safety for
the sake of yours; I'll work by stratagem. Have you

---

[4] The hospital of St. Mary of Bethlehem in London, famous as a
lunatic asylum.

Ha, ha, ha! now comes my turn to be ravished.

courage enough to stand the appearance of 'em?

MRS. SULLEN: Yes, yes, since I have 'scaped your hands, I can face anything.

ARCHER: Come hither, brother Scrub! Don't you know me?

SCRUB: (*almost bursting with relief*) Eh, my dear brother, let me kiss thee. (*runs to Archer and kisses him*)

ARCHER: (*pulling Scrub around to the right side of the bed*) This way — here —

They duck behind the bed just as Gibbet, with a dark lantern in one hand and a pistol in the other, enters cautiously from the left.

GIBBET: Ay, ay, this is the chamber, and the lady alone.

MRS. SULLEN: Who are you, sir? What would you have? D'ye come to rob me?

GIBBET: Rob you! Alack-a-day, madam, I'm only a younger brother, madam; and so, madam, if you make a noise, I'll shoot you through the head; but don't be afraid, madam. (*laying his lantern and pistol upon the table and inspecting the odds and ends of jewelry lying on it*) These rings, madam; don't be concerned, madam, I have a profound respect for you, madam; your keys, madam; don't be frightened, madam; I'm the most of a gentleman. (*searching her pockets and extracting a necklace*) This necklace, madam; I never was rude to any lady; — I have a veneration — for this necklace —

Here Archer, having come around and seized the pistol, takes Gibbet by the collar, trips up his heels, and claps the pistol to his breast.

ARCHER: Hold, profane villain, and take the reward of thy sacrilege!

GIBBET: Oh! Pray, sir, don't kill me; I an't prepared.

ARCHER: How many is there of 'em, Scrub?

SCRUB: Five-and-forty, sir.

ARCHER: Then I must kill the villain, to have him out of the way.

GIBBET: Hold, hold, sir, we are but three, upon my honor.

ARCHER: Scrub, will you undertake to secure him?

SCRUB: Not I, sir; kill him, kill him!

ARCHER: Run to Gipsy's chamber; there you'll find the doctor; bring him hither presently. (*Scrub runs off to the right.*) Come, rogue, if you have a short prayer, say it.

GIBBET: Sir, I have no prayer at all; the government has provided a chaplain to say prayers for us on these occasions.

MRS. SULLEN: Pray, sir, don't kill him: you fright me as much as him.

ARCHER: The dog shall die, madam, for being the occasion of my disappointment. — Sirrah, this moment is your last.

GIBBET: I'll give you two hundred pounds to spare my life.

ARCHER: Have you no more, rascal?

GIBBET: Yes, sir, I can command four hundred, but I must reserve two of 'em to save my life at the sessions.[5]

Scrub returns, leading in Foigard.

ARCHER: Here, doctor, I suppose Scrub and you between you may manage him. Lay hold of him, doctor.

Foigard seizes and holds Gibbet's arms from behind.

GIBBET: What! turned over to the priest already! — Look'ee, doctor, you come before your time; I an't condemned yet, I thank ye.

FOIGARD: Come, my dear joy, I vill secure your body and your shoul too; I vill make you a good Catholic and give you an absolution.

GIBBET: Absolution! Can you procure me a pardon, doctor?

FOIGARD: No, joy.

GIBBET: Then you and your absolution may go to the devil!

ARCHER: Convey him into the cellar; there bind him: — take the pistol, and if he offers to resist, shoot him

---

[5] Trials conducted by justices of the peace.

through the head — and come back to us with all the speed you can.

SCRUB: Ay, ay, come, doctor, do you hold him fast, and I'll guard him.

Foigard drags Gibbet off to the left; Scrub follows with drawn pistol.

ARCHER: In short, madam — (*Feminine shrieking is heard to the right.*) 'Sdeath! The rogues are at work with the other ladies — I'm vexed I parted with the pistol; but I must fly to their assistance. Will you stay here, madam, or venture yourself with me?

MRS. SULLEN: (*taking him by the arm*) Oh, with you, dear sir, with you.

They go off to the right.

SCENE THREE

Another bedchamber in the house, immediately following. Enter from the left Hounslow and Bagshot, with swords drawn, hailing in Lady Bountiful and Dorinda.

HOUNSLOW: Come, come, your jewels, mistress!

BAGSHOT: Your keys, your keys, old gentlewoman!

Aimwell, with drawn sword, dashes in from the right, followed by Cherry.

AIMWELL: Turn this way villains! I durst engage an army in such a cause.

He engages them both.

DORINDA: O madam, had I but a sword to help the brave man!

LADY BOUNTIFUL: (*practically*) There's three or four hanging up in the hall; but they won't draw. I'll go fetch one, however.

She goes off to the right just as Archer and Mrs. Sullen enter from the left.

ARCHER: Hold, hold, my lord! Every man his bird, pray.

They engage man to man; Hounslow and Bagshot are thrown and disarmed.

CHERRY: (aside) What! the rogues taken! Then they'll impeach my father: I must give him timely notice.

She darts off to the right, unobserved in the general excitement.

ARCHER: Shall we kill the rogues?

AIMWELL: No, no, we'll bind them.

ARCHER: Ay, ay. — (to Mrs. Sullen who has taken her place directly beside him after the scuffle) Here, madam, lend me your garter.

MRS. SULLEN: (aside) The devil's in this fellow! He fights, loves, and banters all in a breath. (aloud as she reaches down and picks up a rope) Here's a cord that the rogues brought with 'em, I suppose.

ARCHER: Right, right, the rogue's destiny, a rope to hang himself. (to Aimwell as he binds the highwaymen together) Come, my lord — this is but a scandalous sort of an office, if our adventures should end in this sort of hangman-work; but I hope there is something in prospect that — (He is interrupted by the entrance of Scrub, from the left.) Well, Scrub, have you secured your Tartar?

SCRUB: Yes, sir, I left the priest and him disputing about religion.

AIMWELL: And pray carry these gentlemen to reap the benefit of the controversy.

He delivers the prisoners to Scrub, who leads them out to left. Mrs. Sullen and Dorinda draw together at the left, leaving Archer and Aimwell apart at the right.

MRS. SULLEN: Pray, sister, how came my lord here?

DORINDA: And pray, how came the gentleman here?

MRS. SULLEN: I'll tell you the greatest piece of villainy — (They continue to talk in dumb show while Aimwell and Archer also carry on a private conversation.)

AIMWELL: I fancy, Archer, you have been more successful in your adventures than the housebreakers.

ARCHER: No matter for my adventure; yours is the principal. — Press her this minute to marry you — now while she's hurried between the palpitation of her fear and the joy of her deliverance, now while the tide of her spirits is at high-flood — throw yourself at her feet, speak some romantic nonsense or other — address her, like Alexander in the height of his victory, confound her senses, bear down her reason, and away with her. — The priest is now in the cellar and dare not refuse to do the work.

Lady Bountiful re-enters from the right and joins the two ladies.

AIMWELL: But how shall I get off without being observed?

ARCHER: You a love, and not find a way to get off! — Let me see —

AIMWELL: (*observing a spot of red on Archer's arm*) You bleed, Archer.

ARCHER: (*looking at his arm in surprise*) 'Sdeath, I'm glad on't; this wound will do the business. I'll amuse the old lady and Mrs. Sullen about dressing my wound while you carry off Dorinda.

LADY BOUNTIFUL: (*approaching the two men*) Gentlemen, could we understand how you would be gratified for the services —

ARCHER: (*with stoic severity*) Come, come, my lady, this is no time for compliments; I'm wounded, madam.

LADY BOUNTIFUL, MRS. SULLEN: How! Wounded!

DORINDA: (*to Aimwell*) I hope, sir, you have received no hurt?

AIMWELL: (*blowing her a kiss*) None but what you may cure. (*He moves over to her.*)

LADY BOUNTIFUL: (*to Archer*) Let me see your arm, sir — I must have some powder-sugar to stop the blood. (*examining his arm*) O me! an ugly gash; upon my word, sir, you must go into bed.

ARCHER: Ay, my lady, a bed would do very well. (*to Mrs. Sullen*) Madam, will you do me the favor to conduct me to a chamber.

LADY BOUNTIFUL: Do, do, daughter — while I get the lint and the probe and the plaster ready.

She bustles off to the left. Aimwell suddenly picks up Dorinda in his arms and carries her off to the right.

ARCHER: (*sternly*) Come, madam, why don't you obey your mother's commands?

MRS. SULLEN: How can you, after what is passed, have the confidence to ask me?

ARCHER: And if you go to that, how can you, after what is passed, have the confidence to deny me? Was not this blood shed in your defence, and my life exposed for your protection? Look'ee, madam, I'm none of your romantic fools that fight giants and monsters for nothing; my valour is downright Swiss;[6] I'm a soldier of fortune and must be paid.

MRS. SULLEN: 'Tis ungenerous in you, sir, to upbraid me with your services!

ARCHER: 'Tis ungenerous in you, madam, not to reward 'em.

MRS. SULLEN: How! at the expense of my honor?

ARCHER: Honor! Can honor consist with ingratitude? If you would deal like a woman of honor, do like a man of honor. D'ye think I would deny you in such a case?

Gipsy appears at the left.

GIPSY: Madam, my lady ordered me to tell you that your brother is below at the gate.

MRS. SULLEN: (*as Gipsy retires*) My brother! Heavens be praised! Sir, he shall thank you for your services; he has it in his power.

ARCHER: Who is your brother, madam?

MRS. SULLEN: Sir Charles Freeman. (*moving to the left*) You'll excuse me, sir; I must go and receive him.

She goes off, left.

ARCHER: Sir Charles Freeman! 'Sdeath and hell! my

---

[6] Alluding to the Swiss mercenaries.

old acquaintance. Now unless Aimwell has made good use of his time, all our fair machine goes souse into the sea like the Eddystone.[7]

He goes off to the right.

Back to the drawing-room, a few minutes later. Dorinda enters from the right on Aimwell's arm.

DORINDA: Well, well, my lord, you have conquered; your late generous action will, I hope, plead for my easy yielding; though I must own, your lordship had a friend in the fort before.

AIMWELL: The sweets of Hybla[8] dwell upon her tongue! (*Foigard enters from the left with a service-book open in his hand.*) Here, doctor —

FOIGARD: Are you prepared bote?

DORINDA: I'm ready. But first, my lord, one word. — I have a frightful example of a hasty marriage in my own family; when I reflect upon't, it shocks me. Pray, my lord, consider a little —

AIMWELL: Consider! Do you doubt my honor or my love?

DORINDA: Neither: I do believe you equally just as brave, and were your whole sex drawn out for me to choose, I should not cast a look upon the multitude if you were absent. But, my lord, I'm a woman; colors, concealments may hide a thousand faults in me; therefore know me better first. I hardly dare affirm I know myself in anything except my love.

AIMWELL: (*aside*) Such goodness who could injure! I find myself unequal to the task of villain; she has gained my soul and made it honest like her own. — I cannot, cannot hurt her. (*aloud*) Doctor, retire. (*Foigard goes*

---

[7] The first Eddystone lighthouse, off the port of Plymouth, completed in 1699, was destroyed in a gale in 1703.

[8] A Sicilian town famous for its honey.

off, left.) Madam, behold your lover and your proselyte, and judge of my passion by my conversion! I'm all a lie, nor dare I give a fiction to your arms; I'm all counterfeit, except my passion.

DORINDA: Forbid it, Heaven! A counterfeit!

AIMWELL: I am no lord, but a poor needy man, come with a mean, a scandalous design to prey upon your fortune; but the beauties of your mind and person have so won me from myself that, like a trusty servant, I prefer the interest of my mistress to my own.

DORINDA: Sure I have had the dream of some poor mariner, a sleepy image of a welcome port, and wake involved in storms! Pray, sir, who are you?

AIMWELL: Brother to the man whose title I usurped, but stranger to his honor or his fortune.

DORINDA: (*radiantly*) Matchless honesty! Once I was proud, sir, of your wealth and title, but now am prouder that you want it: now I can show my love was justly levelled, and had no aim but love. (*calling off to left*) Doctor, come in.

Foigard re-enters. Simultaneously, Gipsy comes in from the right and whispers to Dorinda.

DORINDA: (*to Foigard*) Your pardon, sir, we shan't want you now. (*to Aimwell*) Sir, you must excuse me — I'll wait upon you presently.

She goes off to the right with Gipsy.

FOIGARD: (*holding up his hands*) Upon my shoul, now, dis is foolish.

He retires again to the left.

AIMWELL: Gone! and bid the priest depart! It has an ominous look.

Archer enters from the left.

ARCHER: Courage, Tom! Shall I wish you joy?

AIMWELL: (*gloomily*) No.

ARCHER: 'Oons, man, what ha' you been doing?

AIMWELL: O Archer! My honesty, I fear, has ruined me.

ARCHER: How?

AIMWELL: I have discovered myself.

ARCHER: Discovered! And without my consent? What! Have I embarked my small remains in the same bottom with yours, and you dispose of all without my partnership?

AIMWELL: O Archer! I own my fault.

ARCHER: (*bitterly*) After conviction — 'Tis then too late for pardon. You may remember, Mr. Aimwell, that you proposed this folly: as you begun, so end it! Henceforth I'll hunt my fortune single — so farewell! (*turning as if to go*)

AIMWELL: Stay, my dear Archer, but a minute.

ARCHER: Stay! What, to be despised, exposed, and laughed at! No, I would sooner change conditions with the worst of the rogues we just now bound than bear one scornful smile from the proud knight that once I treated as my equal.

AIMWELL: What knight?

ARCHER: Sir Charles Freeman, brother to the lady that I had almost — but no matter for that, 'tis a cursed night's work, and so I leave you to make the best on't. (*starting off again*)

AIMWELL: Freeman! One word, Archer. Still I have hopes; methought she received my confession with pleasure.

ARCHER: (*pausing*) 'Sdeath, who doubts it?

AIMWELL: She consented after to the match; and still I dare believe she will be just.

ARCHER: To herself, I warrant her, as you should have been.

AIMWELL: (*seeing Dorinda about to enter from the right*) By all my hopes she comes, and smiling comes!

DORINDA: (*ecstatically*) Come, my dear lord — I fly with impatience to your arms — the minutes of my absence were a tedious year. Where's this priest?

Foigard dutifully reappears.

ARCHER: 'Oons, a brave girl!

DORINDA: I suppose, my lord, this gentleman is privy to our affairs.

ARCHER: Yes, yes, madam, I'm to be your father.[9]

DORINDA: Come, priest, do your office.

ARCHER: Make haste, make haste, couple 'em any way. (taking Aimwell's hand) Come, madam, I'm to give you —

DORINDA: My mind's altered; I won't.

ARCHER: Eh!

AIMWELL: I'm confounded!

FOIGARD: Upon my shoul, and sho is myshelf.

ARCHER: What's the matter now, madam?

DORINDA: Look'ee, sir, one generous action deserves another. This gentleman's honor obliged him to hide nothing from me; my justice engages me to conceal nothing from him. In short, sir, you are the person that you thought you counterfeited; you are the true Lord Viscount Aimwell, and I wish your Lordship joy. — Now, priest, you may be gone; if my Lord is pleased now with the match, let his Lordship marry me in the face of the world.

AIMWELL, ARCHER: What does she mean?

DORINDA: (as Sir Charles Freeman and Mrs. Sullen enter from the left) Here's a witness for my truth.

SIR CHARLES: My dear Lord Aimwell, I wish you joy.

AIMWELL: Of what?

SIR CHARLES: Of your honor and estate. Your brother died the day before I left London; and all your friends have writ after you to Brussels — among the rest I did myself the honor.

ARCHER: Hark'ee, Sir Knight, don't you banter now?

SIR CHARLES: 'Tis truth, upon my honor.

AIMWELL: (with a tremendous sigh) Thanks to the pregnant stars that formed this accident!

---

[9] In the sense of acting as her father in the marriage ceremony.

ARCHER: Thanks to the womb of time that brought it forth — away with it!

AIMWELL: (*taking Dorinda's hand*) Thanks to my guardian angel that led me to the prize!

ARCHER: And double thanks to the noble Sir Charles Freeman. — My Lord, I wish you joy. Egad, Sir Freeman, you're the honestest fellow living! 'Sdeath, I'm grown strange airy upon this matter! (*to Aimwell*) My Lord, how d'ye? A word, my Lord: don't you remember something of a previous agreement that entitles me to the moiety of this lady's fortune, which I think will amount to five thousand pounds?

AIMWELL: Not a penny, Archer. You would ha' cut my throat just now because I would not deceive this lady.

ARCHER: Ay, and I'll cut your throat again if you should deceive her now.

AIMWELL: (*smiling*) That's what I expected; and to end the dispute, the lady's fortune is ten thousand pounds; we'll divide stakes: take the ten thousand pounds or the lady.

DORINDA: (*flaring up*) How! Is your lordship so indifferent?

ARCHER: No, no, no, madam! His Lordship knows very well that I'll take the money; I leave you to his Lordship, and so we're both provided for.

Count Bellair enters from the left.

COUNT BELLAIR: *Mesdames et Messieurs*, I am your servant trice humble! I hear you be rob here.

AIMWELL: (*quietly*) The ladies have been in some danger, sir.

COUNT BELLAIR: And, begar, our inn be rob too!

AIMWELL: Our inn! By whom?

COUNT BELLAIR: By the landlord, begar! Garzoon, he has rob himself and run away!

ARCHER: Robbed himself!

COUNT BELLAIR: Ay, begar, and me too of a hundre pound.

ARCHER: A hundred pounds?

COUNT BELLAIR: Yes, that I owed him.

AIMWELL: Our money's gone, Frank.

ARCHER: Rot the money! my wench is gone. (*to Count Bellair*) *Savez-vous quelquechose de Mademoiselle Cherry?* [10]

A countryman, in coarse clothing, enters at the left, carrying a strong-box and a letter.

COUNTRYMAN: Is there one Martin here?

ARCHER: Ay, ay — who wants him?

COUNTRYMAN: I have a box here and letter for him.

ARCHER: (*taking the box*) Ha! ha! ha! What's here? Legerdemain! By this light, my lord, our money again! (*opening the letter*) But this unfolds the riddle. (*reading*) Hum, hum, hum! — Oh, 'tis for the public good and must be communicated to the company. (*He reads the letter aloud.*)

> *Mr. Martin,*
>
> *My father, being afraid of an impeachment by the rogues that are taken tonight, is gone off; but if you can procure him a pardon, he'll make great discoveries that may be useful to the country. Could I have met you instead of your master tonight, I would have delivered myself into your hands with a sum that much exceeds that in your strong-box, which I have sent you with an assurance to my dear Martin that I shall ever be his most faithful friend till death.*
>
> Cherry Boniface

There's a billet-doux for you! As for the father, I think he ought to be encouraged; and for the daughter — pray, my Lord, persuade your bride to take her into her service instead of Gipsy.

AIMWELL: I can assure you, madam, your deliverance was owing to her discovery.

---

[10] "Do you know anything of Miss Cherry?"

DORINDA: Your command, my Lord, will do without the obligation. I'll take care of her.

SIR CHARLES: This good company meets opportunely in favor of a design I have in behalf of my unfortunate sister. I intend to part her from her husband. Gentlemen, will you assist me?

ARCHER: Assist you! 'Sdeath, who would not?

COUNT BELLAIR: Assist! Garzoon, we all assist!

Squire Sullen, in a slightly sodden state, comes in from the left.

SQUIRE SULLEN: What's all this? They tell me, spouse, that you had like to have been robbed.

MRS. SULLEN: Truly, spouse, I was pretty near it, had not these two gentlemen interposed.

SQUIRE SULLEN: (*truculently*) How came these gentlemen here?

MRS. SULLEN: That's his way of returning thanks, you must know.

COUNT BELLAIR: Garzoon, the question be apropos for all dat.

SIR CHARLES: You promised last night, sir, that you would deliver your lady to me this morning.

SQUIRE SULLEN: Humph!

ARCHER: Humph! What do you mean by humph? Sir, you shall deliver her. In short, we have saved you and your family; and if you are not civil, we'll unbind the rogues, join with 'em, and set fire to your house. What does the man mean? not part with his wife!

COUNT BELLAIR: Ay, garzoon, de man no understant common justice.

MRS. SULLEN: Hold, gentlemen, all things here must move by consent; compulsion would spoil us. Let my dear and I talk the matter over, and you shall judge it between us.

SQUIRE SULLEN: Let me know first who are to be our judges. (*to Sir Charles*) Pray, sir, who are you?

SIR CHARLES: I am Sir Charles Freeman, come to take away your wife.

SQUIRE SULLEN: (*to Aimwell*) And you, good sir?

AIMWELL: Thomas, Viscount Aimwell, come to take away your sister.

SQUIRE SULLEN: (*to Archer*) And you, pray, sir?

ARCHER: Francis Archer, esquire, come —

SQUIRE SULLEN: To take away my mother, I hope. Gentlemen, you're heartily welcome; I never met with three more obliging people since I was born! (*to Mrs. Sullen*) And now, my dear, if you please, you shall have the first word.

ARCHER: And the last, for five pounds!

MRS. SULLEN: Spouse!

SQUIRE SULLEN: Rib!

MRS. SULLEN: How long have we been married?

SQUIRE SULLEN: By the almanac, fourteen months; but by my account, fourteen years.

MRS. SULLEN: 'Tis thereabout by my reckoning.

COUNT BELLAIR: Garzoon, their account will agree.

MRS. SULLEN: Pray, spouse, what did you marry for?

SQUIRE SULLEN: To get an heir to my estate.

SIR CHARLES: And have you succeeded?

SQUIRE SULLEN: No.

ARCHER: The condition fails of his side. — Pray, madam, what did you marry for?

MRS. SULLEN: To support the weakness of my sex by the strength of his, and to enjoy the pleasures of an agreeable society.

SIR CHARLES: Are your expectations answered?

MRS. SULLEN: No.

COUNT BELLAIR: A clear case! a clear case!

SIR CHARLES: What are the bars to your mutual contentment?

MRS. SULLEN: In the first place, I can't drink ale with him.

SQUIRE SULLEN: Nor can I drink tea with her.

MRS. SULLEN: I can't hunt with you.

SQUIRE SULLEN: Nor can I dance with you.

MRS. SULLEN: I hate cocking[11] and racing.

SQUIRE SULLEN: And I abhor ombre and piquet.[12]

MRS. SULLEN: Your silence is intolerable.

SQUIRE SULLEN: Your prating is worse.

MRS. SULLEN: Have we not been a perpetual offence to each other? a gnawing vulture at the heart?

SQUIRE SULLEN: A frightful goblin to the sight?

MRS. SULLEN: A porcupine to the feeling?

SQUIRE SULLEN: Perpetual wormwood to the taste?

MRS. SULLEN: Is there on earth a thing we could agree in?

SQUIRE SULLEN: Yes — to part.

MRS. SULLEN: With all my heart.

SQUIRE SULLEN: Your hand.

MRS. SULLEN: Here.

SQUIRE SULLEN: These hands joined us, these shall part us. (*dropping her hand and stepping back*) Away!

MRS. SULLEN: (*facing her husband and gesturing to her left*) North.

SQUIRE SULLEN: (*pointing to his left*) South.

MRS. SULLEN: (*pointing behind her*) East.

SQUIRE SULLEN: (*pointing behind him*) West; — far as the poles asunder.

COUNT BELLAIR: Begar, the ceremony be vera pretty!

SIR CHARLES: Now, Mr. Sullen, there wants only my sister's fortune to make us easy.

SQUIRE SULLEN: (*stodgily*) Sir Charles, you love your sister, and I love her fortune; every one to his fancy.

ARCHER: Then you won't refund?

SQUIRE SULLEN: Not a stiver.[13]

ARCHER: Then I find, madam, you must e'en go to your prison again.

COUNT BELLAIR: What is the portion?

---

[11] Cock-fighting.

[12] Ombre, described in Pope's *Rape of the Lock,* was the favorite lady's game in Queen Anne's reign; piquet was the favorite gentleman's game.

[13] A very small Dutch coin.

SIR CHARLES: Ten thousand pounds, sir.

COUNT BELLAIR: Garzoon, I'll pay it, and she shall go home wid me.

ARCHER: Ha! ha! ha! French all over. — Do you know, sir what ten thousand pounds English is?

COUNT BELLAIR: No, begar, no justement.

ARCHER: Why, sir, 'tis a hundred thousand livres.

COUNT BELLAIR: A hundre tousand livres! Ah! garzoon, me canno' do't; your beauties and their fortunes are both too much for me.

ARCHER: Then I will. This night's adventure has proved strangely lucky to us all — for Captain Gibbet in his walk had made bold, Mr. Sullen, with your study and escritoir, and had taken out all the writings of your estate, all the articles of marriage with this lady, bills, bonds, leases, receipts to an infinite value: I took 'em from him, and I deliver 'em to Sir Charles. (*He produces a parcel of papers and parchments from a pocket of his coat and gives it to Sir Charles Freeman.*)

SQUIRE SULLEN: (*clapping his hand to his head*) How, my writings! — my head aches consumedly. Well, gentlemen, you shall have her fortune, but I can't talk. If you have a mind, Sir Charles, to be merry and celebrate my sister's wedding and my divorce, you may command my house — but my head aches consumedly. — Scrub, bring me a dram.

ARCHER: (*to Mrs. Sullen*) Madam, there's a country dance to the trifle that I sung today; your hand, and we'll lead it up. (*The two couples join in a dance.*) 'Twould be hard to guess which of these parties is the better pleased, the couple joined or the couple parted; the one rejoicing in hopes of an untasted happiness and the other in their deliverance from an experienced misery.

> Both happy in their several states we find,
> Those parted by consent, and those conjoined.
> Consent, if mutual, saves the lawyer's fee.
> Consent is law enough to set you free.

Epilogue

(*probably delivered by Mr. Wilks*)

If to our play your judgment can't be kind,
Let its expiring author[1] pity find:
Survey his mournful case with melting eyes,
Nor let the bard be damned before he dies.
Forbear, you fair, on his last scene to frown,
But his true exit with a plaudit crown;
Then shall the dying poet cease to fear
The dreadful knell, while your applause to hear.
At Leuctra so the conquering Theban died,[2]
Claimed his friends' praises, but their tears denied:
Pleased in the pangs of death he greatly thought
Conquest with loss of life but cheaply bought.
The difference this, the Greek was one would fight,
As brave, though not so gay, as Sergeant Kite;[3]
Ye sons of Will's, what's that to those who write?
To Thebes alone the Grecian owed his bays;
You may the bard above the hero raise,
Since yours is greater than Athenian praise.

---

[1] A reference to Farquhar's fatal illness when composing the play.
[2] At the Battle of Leuctra, 371 B.C., the Theban Epaminondas led his troops to victory over the Spartans.
[3] One of the principal characters in Farquhar's *The Recruiting Officer*.

Bibliography

Gellert Spencer Alleman, *Matrimonial Law and the Materials of Restoration Comedy*. Wellingford, Penn., 1942.

Archer, William, *George Farquhar,* in *The Mermaid Series,* edited with an introduction and notes. London: T. Fisher Unwin; New York: Charles Scribner's Sons, 1906.

Frederick S. Boas, *An Introduction to Eighteenth-Century Drama: 1700-1780*. Oxford: The Clarendon Press, 1953.

Willard Connely, *Young George Farquhar — The Restoration Drama at Twilight*. London: Cassell & Co., Ltd., 1949.

Bonamy Dobrée, *Restoration Comedy*. Oxford: The Clarendon Press, 1924. — *English Literature in the Early Eighteenth Century*. New York and London: Oxford University Press, 1959.

Norman N. Holland, *The First Modern Comedies*. Cambridge, Mass.: Harvard University Press, 1959.

Joseph Wood Krutch, *Comedy and Conscience after the Restoration*. New York: Columbia University Press, 1924, 1949.

Martin A. Larson, "The Influence of Milton's Divorce Tracts on Farquhar's *Beaux' Stratagem*." Publications of the Modern Language Association, 1924, VIII.

John Loftis, *Comedy and Society from Congreve to Fielding*. Stanford, Cal.: Stanford University Press, 1959.

Allardyce Nichol, *A History of Early Eighteenth Century Drama, 1700-1750*. Cambridge: University Press, 1925.

John Palmer, *The Comedy of Manners*. London: G. Bell & Sons, Ltd., 1913.

Henry Ten Eyck Perry, *The Comic Spirit in Restoration Drama*. New Haven: Yale University Press; London: Oxford University Press, 1925.

John H. Smith, *The Gay Couple in Restoration Comedy*. Cambridge, Mass.: Harvard University Press, 1948.

Louis A. Strauss, *A Discourse upon Comedy, The Recruiting Officer, The Beaux' Stratagem by George Farquhar*. Boston and London: D. C. Heath & Co., 1914.

Ashley H. Thorndike, *English Comedy*. New York: The Macmillan Company, 1929.

Adolphus William Ward, *A History of English Dramatic Literature*, new and revised edition, 3 vols. London: Macmillan & Co., Ltd.; New York: The Macmillan Company, 1899.

Laurence Whistler, *Sir John Vanbrugh, Architect and Dramatist, 1664-1726*. London: Cobden-Sanderson, 1938.